The Cave of Poison Grass
Essays on the Hannya Sutra

The Cave of Poison Grass
Essays on the Hannya Sutra

by Seikan Hasegawa

Great Ocean Publishers
Arlington, Virginia

The Cave of Poison Grass, Essays on the Hannya Sutra
is the first in a series of books by Seikan Hasegawa
to be published by Great Ocean Publishers.
The books will deal with various subjects, but
their common theme and purpose is that of Zen training:
the practical study of how to live best in each and
every situation. That is why the series is entitled
COMPANIONS OF ZEN TRAINING.

Copyright © 1975 by Seikan Hasegawa

All rights reserved. No part of this book may be used or reproduced in any manner whatsoever without written permission except in the case of brief quotations embodied in critical articles and reviews.

For information write Great Ocean Publishers
738 South 22 St.
Arlington, Virginia 22202

First Printing

Library of Congress Cataloging in Publication Data

Hasegawa, Seikan, 1945-
  The cave of poison grass.

  (Companions of Zen training; 1)
  "The Hannya sutra": p.
  Includes bibliographical references and index.
  1. Prajnaparamitas—Addresses, essays, lectures.
I. Prajnaparamitas. English. 1975. II. Title. III. Series.
BQ1887.H37   294.3'8   75-6600

ISBN 0-915556-00-6 (Hardcover)
      0-915556-01-4 (Paperback)

Manufactured in the United States of America

Contents

	Preface	1
I	The Hannya Sutra	4
II	The Meaning of the Title	8
III	The Bodhisattva Way	29
IV	Why We Suffer	80
V	Emptiness	92
VI	$X \gtreqless Y$	108
VII	Inviolable Being	118
VIII	Active Understanding of Mu	123
IX	Where Humanity Arises	134
X	Freedom, The Life of No Attainment	146
XI	Anuttara-samyak-sambodhi	157
	Notes	166
	Indexes	177

Illustrations

Nansen About to Cut the Cat   13

Kyogen Getting Enlightenment   26
   Ichi geki shochi o bozu
   Sara ni shuji o karazu
   (One blow made me forget all discrimination
   No need any more to train to be perfect)

Training Monks on Pilgrimage   47

Bodhidharma Coming from India to China   58

Poem: *Kaze fukedomo ugokazu*   91
   Tenpen no tsuki
   (Though the wind blows, the moon in the
   boundless sky does not move)
   Calligraphy by Bundo Hasegawa

The Sixth Patriarch Working   115

Bodhidharma, with the Calligraphy *Bussho*   143
   (Buddha Nature)
   Painting by Hakuin

Butsu (Buddha)   159

All illustrations, including the cover, are by Seikan Hasegawa, with the exception of the paintings by Bundo Hasegawa and Hakuin, from the collection of Seikan Hasegawa.

Preface

**There are many people who know the Way,
but there are few who practice it.**[1]

This phrase is not mocking or cruelly criticizing us. It is the lamentation of a merciful person of wisdom upon seeing us and determining to continue helping us.

Indeed, though most people have been taught to read, how much have they sharpened their ability to read between the lines or to see suchness[2] itself before they read? Intelligence is useful for judging after something has happened, but it has no power to create.

"Human being, be ambitious!"[3] Will you not hear these words sometimes in your inner ear? Eating food is an important matter, but which will you choose: to be served delicious food with insults, or to be served plain food with a full welcome? We are not animals but human beings. Why shouldn't we be ambitious to live in the spiritual world, not only in the material world?

During the seventeenth century in Japan, even the highest class, the samurai,[4] often could not read. Of course peasants were far from educated. But there was a peasant's daughter named Tsuna. She was only fourteen years old and employed as a nursemaid to a samurai family. One day while she was carrying a baby on her back in the garden, a wolf entered with teeth bared. She quickly put her baby on the ground and covered him with her body. People heard a sound and came into the garden. After chasing away the wolf they gathered her up. She was bleeding all over and her warm blood soaked into the earth. She asked only, "How is baby . . . ?" and died before receiving an answer. Then people saw the unhurt, smiling baby beneath her body.

What could she do at that time as a little girl? What would we do if we were she? How much have we progressed since her time? In old times there were many such cases.

Really we should realize we are spiritual beings. There is more than material or intelligence. On the mountain highlands there is clean air and beautiful flowers.

Spring, 1972
At Rock Creek

The Stanza for Opening The Sutras
Kai-kyō-ge[1]

The unsurpassed, profoundly deep, fine, wonderful Law
Difficult to meet with in hundreds of thousands of kalpas,
Now I can see and hear, accept and hold it;
My only hope is to grasp the real meaning of the Tathagatha.

The Stanza for Lecturing on
The *Hannya-shin-gyō*[2]

Even though I am a stutterer to preach the Law
How can I lock myself in a dark room behind wild grasses
While all parents and children are working hard
   and crying in the field!

As sorrowful as parents with no child is the priest with no laymen,
With no harmony in the contradictions of life.
And who does not want to live and die on the Cross?

Ask neither to misty past nor to hazy future,
But see just now and here,—the spirit of friendship!
All things come out from the soil and return to it,
   then who are you?

I The Hannya Sutra

Maka-hannya-haramita-shin-gyō is a compendium or summary of the *Mahāprajñāpāramitā Sūtra*[1] and consists of only one page. We call this sutra *Hannya-shin-gyō* or *Shin-gyō* for short. There is no other sutra which is spread as widely in Japan. All Buddhists, whatever their sect, will chant this sutra on every religious occasion.[2]

From the time I was a baby I heard the Hannya-shin-gyo from my mother's mouth as a lullaby. In the Zen monastery I chanted this sutra almost ten times a day.

Why, among so many sutras, has the Hannya-shin-gyo become so popular? The most important reason is that the virtue and grace of this sutra is most excellent and since old times it was propagated by various sage persons.[3] The second reason is that all the principles of Buddhism were included without any omission within quite a short sutra, the number of Chinese characters being only two hundred and seventy-two. Third, in this sutra, *Avalokiteśvara*[4] appears. Therefore when people have worship to Avalokitesvara they respect the Hannya-shin-gyo as well. Fourth, this sutra has a good rhythm for chanting. And fifth is a general tendency of the Japanese to emulate any distinguished person. In fact, most people who chant or hear this sutra now don't know even its literal meaning.

Originally this sutra was written in Sanskrit. I can understand Sanskrit only a little and so use Chinese translation. Scholars say that the seven Chinese translations and the one Tibetan translation came from the same Sanskrit text. Among the Chinese translations, the two translations by Kumārajīva and by Hsüan-chuang are the most often read. An English translation has been made by Dr. D.T. Suzuki in his *Manual of Zen Buddhism*.[5] Now I would like to lecture about Hsuan-chuang's Hannya-shin-gyo using my English translation.

Hsuan-chuang was a great Chinese priest of the T'ang Dynasty. He was born in 600 A.D. south of the Yellow River and when he was quite young he entered Dai-jion-ji (Great Merciful Kindness Temple). He studied the Abhidharma and Vijñaptimatrata philosophies of Buddhism. While studying these he determined to get the original Sanskrit texts for himself. He started from China in 629 for India via Central Asia and Afghanistan. At that time he was thirty years old. Finally he reached middle India and could visit that land which is the holy land for Buddhists.[6] He became a disciple of the scholar Śīlabhadra, at Nālanda Temple, and studied for ten years under him.

Though I write this as if he were an utter stranger to me, I know that even in modern days it is an unspeakably difficult and dangerous thing to travel in such a place. I went to take training in Southern Buddhism in a Thailand temple. I had no money. Since I was a Buddhist priest I could not do any shameful conduct, such as irresponsible young people often do. Throwing the mud in the Buddha's face is the most cruel nonsense for us. Whenever I was suffering by illness, lack of food or money, difficulty in speaking, difference of temperature, and so on, I could comfort myself by thinking of Reverend Hsuan-chuang.

In 645 he came back to China with the manuscripts of six hundred and fifty-seven Sanskrit texts and many Buddha images, as well as some relics of Śākyamuni Buddha. After returning, Hsuan-chuang, with the help of about three thousand disciples, translated one thousand three hundred and thirty-three volumes of sutras which established a new epoch in the history of the translation of Buddhist sutras. His translation is called "the new translation" *(shin-yaku)* as distinguished from the old one *(ku-yaku)* by Kumarajiva.

Among his translations the largest work was the translation of the Mahaprajnaparamita Sutra. Nowadays in the monastery we read this sutra aloud at the beginning of each season to pray for the peace of the world and the prosperity of Buddhism for the happiness of all people, to increase the faith of the people, and to be free of all illness or bad mind which might interfere with our training. Usually only the titles of the sutra and the titles of the chapters are read. This ceremony is also very useful to protect the pages from book worms.

The essence of this great sutra is the Hannya-shin-gyo, two hundred seventy-two characters in length.[7]

At first I will give the romanized transliteration of the Chinese as it is chanted in Japan and then my English translation from the Chinese.

MAKA-HANNYA-HARAMITA-SHIN-GYO

Kan ji zai bo sa, gyo jin han nya ha ra mi ta ji, sho ken go un kai ku, do its sai ku yaku.

Sha ri shi, shiki fu i ku, ku fu i shiki, shiki soku ze ku, ku soku ze shiki. Ju so gyo shiki yaku bu nyo ze.

Sha ri shi, ze sho ho ku so, fu sho fu metsu, fu ku fu jo, fu zo fu gen.

Ze ko ku chu mu shiki, mu ju so gyo shiki, mu gen ni bi zets shin ni, mu shiki sho ko mi soku ho, mu gen kai nai shi mu i shiki kai, mu mu myo, yaku mu mu myo jin, nai shi mu ro shi, yaku mu ro shi jin, mu ku shu metsu do, mu chi yaku mu toku,i mu sho toku ko.

Bo dai sats ta, e han nya ha ra mi ta ko, shin mu ke ge, mu ke ge ko, mu u ku fu, on ri its sai ten do mu so, ku gyo ne han.

San ze sho butsu, e han nya ha ra mi ta ko, toku a noku ta ra sam myaku sam bo dai, ko chi han nya ha ra mi ta, ze dai jin shu, ze dai myo shu, ze mu jo shu, ze mu to do shu, no jo its sai ku, shin jitsu fu ko, ko setsu han nya ha ra mi ta shu, soku setsu shu watsu, gya tei, gya tei, ha ra gya tei, hara so gya tei bo dhi so wa ka.

Han nya shin gyo.

MAHA-PRAJNA-PARAMITA-HRDAYA-SUTRA

When the Bodhisattva Avalokitesvara practiced the deep Prajna-paramita, he perceived that the Five Skandhas are all empty and was freed from all sufferings.

My Sariputra, form is no different from emptiness, emptiness is no different from form; form is emptiness as itself and emptiness is form as itself. The same can be said of sensation, thought, volition, and consciousness.

My Sariputra, this empty form of all Dharmas can not be born and not be ruined, not be polluted and not be purified, and not be increased and not be decreased. Therefore in emptiness there is not form, sensation, thought, volition, and consciousness; and not eyes, nose, tongue, body, and mind; and not matter, sound, smell, taste, touch, and laws; and not the world of eyes, . . . until the world of consciousness. There is not ignorance, and not the end of ignorance, . . . until not old age and death, and not the end of old age and death; there is not suffering, accumulation, annihilation, and the way; there is not wisdom, and not attainment because there is not that which can be attained.

Bodhisattva has no obstacles in his mind, because he is living in the Prajna-paramita, and he has no fears because there are no obstacles; he has gone far beyond the delusions and illusions, and perfected Nirvana.

All Buddhas of the three worlds live in Prajna-paramita; therefore they get the Anuttara-samyak-sambodhi. Therefore we should know the Prajna-paramita is the great mysterious Mantram, the great wisdom Mantram, the great supreme Mantram, the great peerless Mantram which can remove all sufferings very well; it is truth but not falsehood. Then there is the Mantram of Prajna-paramita. It said, "Gate, gate, paragate, parasamgate, bodhi, svaha!"

II The Meaning of the Title

Maka-hannya-haramita-shin-gyo

Mahā-prajñā-pāramitā-hṛdaya-sūtra

The title of the sutra always expresses its contents with great clarity. In present-day bookshops there are many books with titles having little relation to their contents. This is not true of sutras. Let me stop on the way to give a few examples. There is the *Kegon-kyō*, in full title *Daihōkō-butsu-kegon-kyō*. This sutra is the backbone of the culture of the Nara Dynasty[1] in Japan. It describes the enlightened world of Sakyamuni who became Buddha. *Dai* means "great," and *hōkō* means "long and wide world," which combined mean limitless world, the world of truth. *Butsu* means "Buddha." *Kegon* means "decorated with flowers," which is a metaphor for the trainer who walks on the Bodhisattva Way. Sakyamuni was a child of human beings, but he reached the world of truth by his walking on the Bodhisattva Way. Buddha's enlightened world is described in this Kegon-kyo. *Kyō* means "sutra."

For this Kegon-kyo there is a complementary sutra which is named *Hokke-kyō;* in full title, *Myōhō-renge-kyō*. It is said that the culture of the Heian Dynasty[2] was the culture of Hokke-kyo. Kegon-kyo speaks of Buddha, but Hokke-kyo speaks of the Law which is not relative but eternal, unchangeable, absolute, universal Law. This Law is covered with dust, is buried in our mind like a diamond in a stone. But still it will not be polluted by anything. Therefore this Wonderful Law was compared to the lotus flower. *Myōhō* means "Wonderful Law," and *renge* means "lotus flower." But why was this lotus flower chosen to describe the Law of Sakyamuni Buddha? In the *Yuima-kyō* it was said that the lotus flower does not grow in the highlands or mountains. Lotus flowers don't bloom in the beautiful mountain, nor in in the clean field. Always they bloom only in the dirty, muddy field. New York is quite a good place for the person who likes to live beautifully.

By the way, another peculiarity of the lotus flower is that it has both its bloom and fruit at the same time. Other flowers have fruit after their blooming has finished. Our Mahayana Buddhism is like this lotus. No one can find the correct enlightenment when they cut off their worldy passions. The flower of enlightenment blooms in the midst of worldly passions. And there is no enlightenment even if we finish our training of the Bodhisattva Way. Our training has no end. There is the fruit which is enlightenment only while we are training. Or we can say, when we begin our training already there is enlightenment. Many people are misunderstanding about this point. They think they can get enlightenment after a certain period of training. I should say that is not enlightenment but falling into the Hell of dark ignorance. Especially in America, I have noticed, somehow many good people superstitiously believe in the importance of such decorative titles as *Roshi* (Zen Master) and *Inka-shomei* (certification of enlightenment). Such honorary titles have no relationship with the training of the Bodhisattva Way or enlightenment. To this I will refer later. Meanwhile, here is an interesting story related to the lotus flower.

> In Southern Japan there was a Zen priest named Musan.
> Though he came from a very poor peasant family, he was recognized by a lord. All the neighboring samurais did not enjoy seeing cheap inferiors taking a higher seat than their own.
> A samurai wanted to put Priest Musan to shame in public. During a drinking party this samurai offered the priest an alcohol cup saying, "How are you, The Peasant of Kushira Village?"
> Everyone watched this scene to see what would happen. But Priest Musan was very calm, and smiling he said only one phrase:

"The lotus flower in the muddy pond."
From this time most people began to admire and respect him.

Now I will explain the title Maka-hannya-haramita-shin-gyo. *Maka* is not added in Hsuan-chuang's Hannya-shin-gyo. But generally in the social world people add Maka. When we begin to chant, if there is this Maka it makes a much better sound than beginning with Hannya. Literally Maka, in Sanskrit *Maha*, has three meanings: "great," "many," and "excellent." But even though I translate it literally, your understanding of Maka will not be helped. "Great" does not always mean "many," and "many" is not necessarily "great." Like these, Maka has many wide meanings (and even if I explain literally you will only become confused). This Maka is really the essence of Sakyamuni Buddha. In my understanding, Maka means our mind, which is the origin of the universe. Mind has no beginning or end and it is everywhere, always. Seeking to get this mind, we only come to the final conclusion that we cannot get it.

Bodhidharma, the First Patriarch of the Zen sect in China, came from India (in 520 ?). He was the Twenty-eighth Patriarch in India according to tradition.[3]

Jinko (487-593) was a very wise person since childhood and as a philosopher he studied all of Confucianism, Taoism, and Buddhism. But still he was not satisfied about the basic question: What is my being? What is my mind finally? Who am I?

Just at this juncture he heard that Bodhidharma had brought the Buddha-mind seal[4] and was staying at Shorin Temple doing zazen (sitting meditation) facing the wall every day.

It was on a snowy evening, December ninth, that Jinko visited Bodhidharma. But Bodhidharma did not allow Jinko to enter his room. Jinko stood in the snowfall all through the night to get permission of discipleship.

But Bodhidharma said, "The Buddha Way will not be attained with easy determination. Going home quickly is better for you." Jinko was overcome with concern and at last he cut off his left arm and presented it to Bodhidharma as an expression of his sincere mind to seek the Way. Finally Bodhidharma let him stay as a disciple and gave him a new name: Eka.[5]

Eka was living in the chaotic darkness, not knowing what was his mind. Then he asked to Bodhidharma, "My teacher, I don't feel any satisfaction. Please let me be satisfied."

Bodhidharma replied, "I see. I will satisfy you. Please bring your unsatisfied mind to me."

Eka was an honest and pure trainer and looked for his unsatisfied mind for dear life. He was already a great scholar. He must have tried to find his unsatisfied mind in various directions. His body and spirit became a lump of doubt. But he could not find any unsatisfied mind.

Then he said to Bodhidharma, "Though I sought the unsatisfied mind sincerely, there is no such thing."

Bodhidharma said to him, "Already I satisfied you."

Really Eka could understand that originally there is no such thing. He had been in suffering which he made by himself. He recognized the mind.

Maka is this mind. If we think that this mind is an eternal thing, we will fall into *Jo-ken* which is "the view of the eternal." 'All things are changing' is the first truth of Buddhism. And in this Law there is no exception. Therefore if people think that this universe is eternal and that our spirit also will not die though our bodies die, and that they will continue to live somehow in some place, they are not Buddhist. But on the contrary, if we think that all things are empty or that there is no existence at all, then we must fall into *Dan-ken*, "the view of nothingness." 'All things are depending on Cause and Effect' is the second truth of Buddhism. The opinion that the soul is immortal is Jo-ken; nihilism is Dan-ken. Buddha showed us the Middle Way, apart from both edges of *U* (being), and *Mu* (nothingness).

Our mind is not only beast and not only God. Whenever we try to grasp it with our words and our thinking, mind will go away. It is just like hunting a bird for research: if we shoot it and bring it into the study room, it is no longer a bird, but rather something like the dust of a bird. If we would like to know what a bird is, we must see it in the forest while it is living. Most Zen *koans*,[6] though they seem impossible to understand because of their paradoxical direct touching with reality, are talking about our mind. If you see koans in this way, you can be much closer to them. For instance, there is the following koan about Zenji Nansen:[7]

> One day the head monks from east and west zendos (meditation halls) were arguing about a cat. Then Priest Nansen grasped it suddenly and held it up, saying: "All of you, tell me one suitable word for the Way of Zen. If you do, I will help this cat. If you cannot say, I will kill it." No one could reply. Therefore Priest Nansen cut it.

The cat means our mind. The cat should be understood while it is living. This mind cannot be caught by any dualistic thought; mind is not U, not Mu, not sound, not color, nameless, formless. It is a really strange but wonderful thing and working very well.

>   A cloud has no mind
>   And it leaves from the harbor.

We name this mind Maka. If a person understands the deep meaning of Maka, he understands the essence of Sakyamuni Buddha.

Here, before I go on with my interpretation, I would like to introduce to you the old principles for the translation of Buddhist sutras. They were made in China by Hsuan-chuang. We call these principles "the five kinds of untranslatable words," *Goshu-fuhon*. First of all, we will not translate the words which have profound meanings, in order to encourage good usage and avoid bad usage. One good example is *Hannya* (*Prajñā* in Sanskrit). In English this will be found translated as "wisdom," with its synonyms "wit," "sense," "intelligence," "prudence," "sagacity." But all of these can have alternate meanings, good or bad, such as bad wisdom. Bad wisdom is unnecessary for our lives. With the progress of culture,

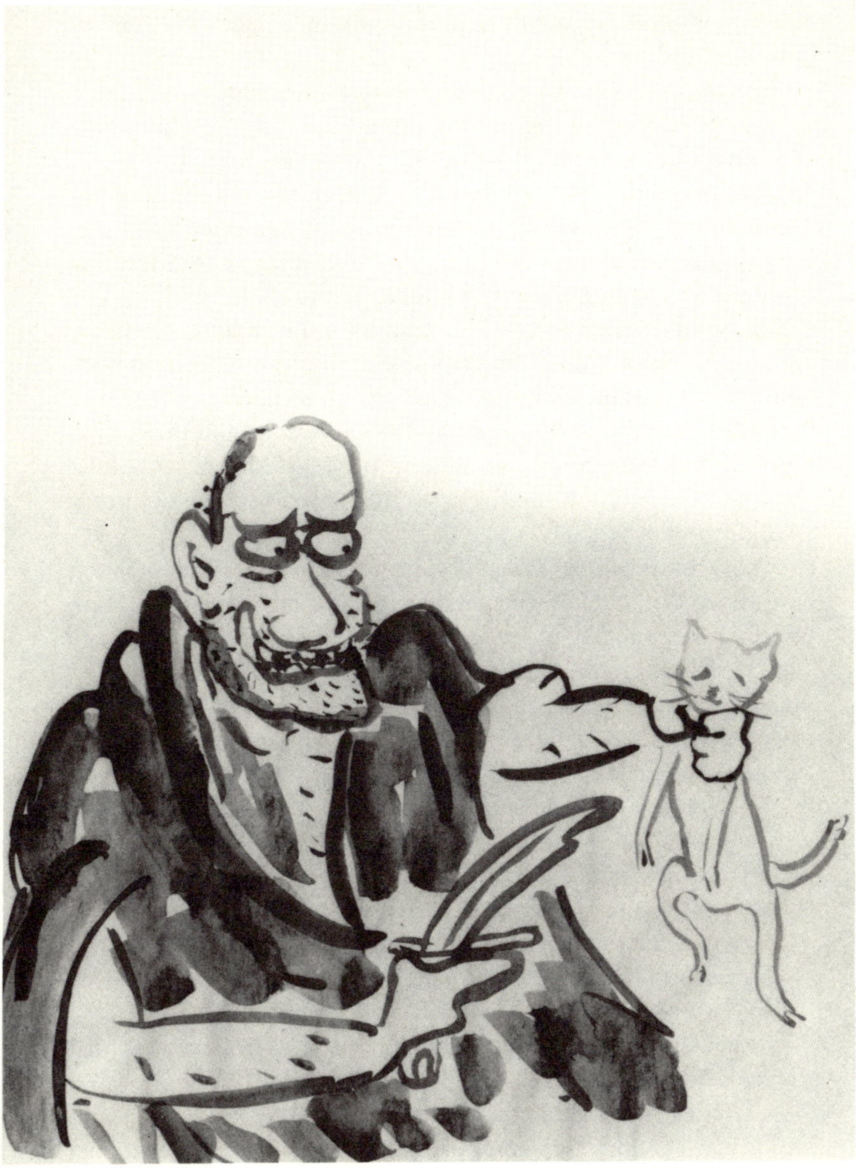

intellectual offenses are increasing. Then we cannot agree that all wisdom is good. Children and parents are often fighting because of this bad wisdom.

Hannya is not such a kind of wisdom. It is to enlighten people from losing the human way, to intuit the great life which is in all of the universe. Therefore this Hannya will not be translated, in order to avoid the creation of bad wisdom and to continue the creation of good wisdom. The Sanskrit word has been assimilated into Japanese, though Zen priests sometimes use it very ironically or incorrectly as *Hannya to,* "boiling water of wisdom," for alcohol.

The second reason we don't translate a word is because of its many meanings. Maka is an example of this kind of word. If we use one possible translation for it, the word "great," we limit its meaning to something relative. Even great can have several meanings as in the proverb "A great city is a great desert." But Maka should not be used in such a relative, comparative sense. It is beyond any contradictory world.

Third, mystic words (*dhāranī*) will not be translated. These dharani are secret. Without knowing their literal meanings, if we chant them sincerely we can enter into *sanmai* (*samādhi*) which is the situation we get by concentration of mind and body on a single object until after the contrast of subject and object has disappeared. Our mind will be studied progressively deeper in reflection, concentration, *Dhyana,* and finally samadhi.

I once heard the following story by a Westerner:

Once upon a time there was a young man thirsty for knowledge. He went to a city in Egypt to seek true wisdom. There he eagerly searched, but finding it was not so easy. One day he sat down with his teacher in a quiet, secret room. There was a huge statue covered with a fine white silk, standing as if solemnity itself.

Suddenly this young man asked his teacher, "What is that statue?"

"That is the Truth!" the teacher answered.

Hearing this, the young man was surprised and cried out

involuntarily with great joy, "Here it was hidden! Always I was looking for this truth!"

At that time the teacher gravely warned the young man, "No one should remove this cover with human, dirty, sinful hands until God himself takes it off."

But the young man was worried and could not easily give up even though he tried and tried. In the middle of the night he stole into the room in which the statue was standing. The statue covered with the fine white silk was shining with silver color in the pale moonlight which came through the high window of a cupola. Over and over again he hesitated. Finally he determined to take the cover off. What did he see?

Next morning people found a young man lying with colorless face under the statue which was covered with fine white silk. The young man had become a cold corpse. His tongue did not utter his experience, the thing he had seen, eternally.

This story explains very well why we don't translate the secret words, dharani. If you really train in the Way, gradually you can understand this kind of matter, even though at the moment you feel it is a strange kind of superstition or something else. Real religion is the real science more than science.

The fourth kind of word which we don't translate is by custom or well-established precedent left untranslated. An example is *Anokutara-sammyaku-sambodai* (*Anuttara-samyak-saṃbodhi* in Sanskrit). This phrase means "perfect enlightenment," or "the unsurpassed wisdom of the Buddhas." Since ancient times it hasn't been translated and we use it as it is in our language.

It was used even in the *waka*, the Japanese poem form of thirty-one syllables. Daishi Dengyo (also known as Saicho, 767-822), who founded the Japanese Tendai Sect of Buddhism at Hiei Mountain, left this poem for us:

> All Buddhas of Anokutara-sammyaku-sambodai,
> Divinely protect this reforested Hiei Mountain
> On which I am standing!

Fifth, words which have meanings foreign to Chinese are not translated, such as *bodai-ju* (*bodhi-vṛkṣa*) or *sara so-ju* (*śāla*). These are the names of trees which grow in India. Therefore we cannot do more than transliterate them.

These five are called Goshu-fuhon, the five kinds of untranslatable words. I hope translators of religious cultures will take care when they work. Otherwise good people must get cheap imports. Furthermore, they will lose the chance to understand the correct Way. In my experience of staying in America, sorrowfully I must say that I have found most translations from Zen words to be incorrect, particularly where those words are used in speech. "Lecture" and *teisho* are completely different, just as different as "dialogue" and *sanzen*.[8]

The titles *Zenji* and *Roshi,* are also usually mistranslated. Zenji means, literally, Teacher of Zen. In Japan Zenji generally is used for the highly-trained priest of the Zen sect. But, in fact, in one sutra (*Zen-ju-i-ten-shi-sho-mon-kyō*) there is the following explanation about Zenji:

> The Ten-shi, (a king) asked to Monju Bodhisattva, "What kind of priest is worthy of being called Zenji?"
> Monju Bodhisattva replied, "The priest who doesn't separate his thinking and acting in any *Dharma*. That is, the one who is not born. Such a priest is worthy of being called Zenji."

Zenji is the respectable name for the priest who is not living in the dualistic, discriminating world regardless of the situation, but lives as suchness, in the suchness which is Law, truth itself. It is very difficult to live in this way. In this sense I am not worthy of being called Zenji.

"Zen Master" is supposed to be the translation for the Japanese, *Roshi*. *-Shi* and *-ji* are the same, both meaning "teacher." *Ro* means literally "old age." In China and Japan old people were respected. Then for such respectable persons we will use this Ro. Therefore,

Roshi means sometimes "old teacher," and sometimes "respectable teacher." But modern Japanese somehow use Roshi for the Zen trainer who has been certified by his teacher as an enlightened person. It is rather the result of the influence of the social world on the religious world. I must say, as it is used in the modern world it is quite a low word. Because it is used as a kind of human rank or title which is a matter of the social world. Sometimes there is a Roshi who is not a Zenji.[9]

The translation of religious culture is difficult and responsible work. For those who do such work, love and respect for human beings are more necessary than any skills. If someone without real training and without enlightened eye translates or writes about religion, his work only confuses good people and separates them from the treasure of the Law. Good people also, I hope, don't depend on such untrustable letters after recognizing the necessity of training. Religious training is not in the letters.

I shall go on with my interpretation continuing with the word Hannya (Prajna). In Western philosophy Hannya will be described by the word "truth" which is "universal validity," and "necessity," or "transcendental wisdom," or in Western religion "God." Though these words are difficult to understand objectively, when we see the mind which created these words, understanding will be much easier. Hannya is the word of admiration for our virtue of natural being and its free working which each person has already since he was born. Freely our eyes see the colors, ears hear the sounds, nose smells the fragrances, tongue tastes the flavors, body feels the materials, brain thinks phenomena. Though all of these organs are not facing their objects with any special care, still they can recognize. These we have already, before we try to get them; they are really naturally being and working freely. We have such great, wonderful virtue. Therefore this virtue was called Hannya. For awakening, enlightening ourselves, at first we should be aware of these treasures and not seek outside of ourselves. There is the Way in the near place. Otherwise, even though we shine outside like a lighthouse, inside is dark. Instead of chasing knowledge which comes from outside, we must study ourselves. And continue to study until realizing finally "who am I?", "what is my original face before my father and mother were born?" This is the only correct way to reach the life of religious training. Until we reach this step, whether we go on pilgraimage or just wander, religious training will not begin.

Like this, everyone has Hannya enough, but by their so-called *funbetsu,* "discrimination," so often they are blindfolding their Hannya. Hannya itself is not bad, not good. It is beyond any contradictory, mutual contrast. It is like a diamond which is hiding in the dust. Our discrimination, is making dust. Water itself is neither good nor bad; but if a snake drinks it, it will become poison and if a cow drinks it, it will become milk. Our discrimination makes categories: bad or good, Buddha or ignorant persons, hungry ghosts, beasts. They are just various things coming in front of a bright mirror: all things are reflected as their own color. If you stand in front of the mirror with bad discrimination, you will be reflected as a bad person; if you stand with beautiful discrimination, you will be reflected as a beautiful person. The mirror, Hannya itself, however, will not get any color or feeling from you or any object. An atomic bomb itself is not good or bad. It depends on how people will use it, with what kind of discrimination. If you have red sunglasses everything will become red and with green glasses all will be seen as green. Communists have glasses of their own color and Capitalists have theirs, though both are seeing the same thing. All fighting arises from this discrimination. If people understand this once and for all, they must take off their own glasses called "-ism," "contention," "position," and so on. And see as suchness, with Hannya eye which is every man's mind. If we can see Hannya we can understand the saying of the Kegon-kyo: "Mind and Buddha and all sentient beings are not different, three are one."

When we can understand that all thinking, discrimination, is illusion, then it is a valuable thing and we can use it for people's happiness. Many people are making suffering for others and for themselves because they do not know this. We say they are defiled with the three poisons: covetousness, anger, and delusion. Utimately all sufferings come from these three poisons. Occasionally these poisons appear from our mind. But if you examine these intimately, you can understand they have no selves, no real existence. Then if you are not blinded with these poisons, you will be free from any suffering and have no need to make others suffer as well. Your mind is originally Hannya itself, you also have Buddha nature. That's why Zenji Hakuin said, "We sentient beings are all originally Buddhas."[10] And you will also realize that in this world there is not a thing unworthy of being.

> One day Monju Bodhisattva asked his attendant, trainer Zenzai:
> "Bring to me a thing which has no worth."
> In response, trainer Zenzai looked all over the world. But at last he came back and reported:
> "There was not a thing which has no worth in this world."
> "I see. If that's so then please bring me something which has worth."
> As soon as trainer Zenzai heard these words, he picked up a piece of grass at his feet.

"Only a small brain makes things worthless," and "For a good doctor, all grasses are medicine" are Japanese proverbs which speak very well. But you should know honestly, politely, that without religious training you cannot get this Hannya eye. By reading books you will get only knowledge and discrimination and if you are lucky you will realize the necessity of training. I hope you can train earlier by even a day and testify your understanding in your actual life. Living such a life is performing the real humanity, not dreaming it only in your brain. But religious training to become aware of Hannya eye, enlightenment, is not so easy for everyone to do. Why is it so difficult? Because it is not a matter of getting anything formally. Quite the opposite, it is throwing off everything one time. If you have no deep love for all sentient beings, give up the wish to train and instead work sincerely in each occupation, which is a little better use of your life. And if you work very well, even for your money, that is good for all people even though you cannot see why.

The above is an explanation of Hannya. Since old times Buddhist scholars explained Hannya by three divisions: *Jisso-hannya,* "the Prajna (wisdom) inherent in all sentient beings"; *Kansho-hannya,* "the Prajna of observation"; and *Moji-hannya,* "the Prajna of letters." Jisso-hannya means the great truth in this universe from which all phenomena in this world are created and progressing. Even a flower or a butterfly is the form which came from the great universal truth which is the mercy of Buddha. Then everything is showing us the Way, Hannya, of the universe everywhere.

Nevertheless, people have on the colored glasses of delusion, illusion. Therefore they cannot see truth itself as suchness, most of the time. But if they see anything with the Buddha's light, they can see the respectable Buddha even in a drop of water, even in a blade of grass. This correct observation of the origin of all phenomena as suchness we call Kansho-hannya.

Moji-hannya means scriptures which were written about Hannya such as the Shin-gyo, or in this case, my book.

Next I will talk about *Haramita.* This word comes from the Sanskrit, *Pāramitā.* It will not be translated, only transliterated. It is also written with two t's: Haramitta. However, I was born in Kyoto and trained in middle Japan and there people pronounce it Haramita. Therefore I write it as "Haramita." Paramita signifies "the situation of reaching the other shore," or "the one who reached the other shore." This means to enter from the suffering, delusive world which is called *kleśa* to the satisfied, enlightened world, called *Nirvāṇa.*

Rinzai is considered the founder of the Rinzai Sect of Zen Buddhism in China.[11] His temple stood facing a river, and his name comes from this fact combined with the sense of Haramita. The name Rinzai means "to help people to cross the river."

When we cross over the river there is a difference between crossing alone and crossing with many people. Quite naturally from this difference the distinction of *Mahāyāna* and *Hīneyāna* appeared.

Hineyana means a small vehicle, such as a bicycle by which only one person can go to his destination. Mahayana is a large vehicle, such as a train. Of course, the purpose of Buddhism is Mahayana: to go to the enlightened world along with all sentient beings. Furthermore, if we think only of human beings without caring about the animals or trees, that must be called Hineyana. A Bodhisattva realizes that without others' happiness there is no happiness for him also. Then he must get enlightenment for himself and for all others, and until all sentient beings get enlightenment to enter Nirvana he vows he will not enter into Nirvana.

One ideal Buddhist layman was Vimalakīrti.[12] He became ill and many great Bodhisattvas visited his bed. To Monju Bodhisattva's question, "Why did you become ill?" Vimalakirti answered, "Because all sentient beings are ill, therefore I am."

Indeed, if a child becomes ill his parents also cannot enjoy; that is why they are parents. For Buddhism there are no foreigners, strangers; all sentient beings are with Bodhisattvas. The practice of Buddhism is done by these Bodhisattvas. Without Bodhisattvas Buddhism would become only an idealistic philosophy. If we do not have a Bodhisattva in ourselves, our understanding of Buddhism also is an idealistic philosophy.

While I am talking about Mahayana and Hineyana I would like to correct some people's misunderstanding that Mahayana Buddhism describes the Buddhism of the North, such as Tibet, Korea, China and Japan, and Hineyana Buddhism describes that of the Southern countries Thailand, Burma, Sri Lanka and so on. If you consider what I have said, you can understand that the difference between Mahayana and Hineyana is not determined by place but only by the practice of Bodhisattvas. During my stay in a Thailand temple as a training monk, I saw there were many great Bodhisattvas, and in Japan I can find many Hineyana Buddhists. If some priest speaks of the Hineyana in reference to Southern Buddhism, he is only proving he is not qualified as a Mahayana Buddhist. Furthermore, for designating Southern Buddhism now we have the correct name which is Theravada Buddhism.

Then now I shall talk of the actual meanings of Haramita. Haramita means reaching the other shore of not-be-born, not-be-ruined, which is Nirvana. Each person should know this truth by himself like the person who knows the coldness or warmth of water by drinking it. Know and do not be deluded by the vision of life and death. Why do people admit the vision of life and death? Because they admit the existence of their body; not only that, they think their body is theirs. If their body is really theirs, why can't they use it as they like? In fact they must become ill and they must die even if they don't want to. In the Christian Gospel according to Saint Matthew (5:34) the following sentences were written: "But I say unto you, swear not at all; neither by heaven, for it is the throne of God; nor by the earth, for it is the footstool of his feet; nor by Jerusalem, for it is the city of the great King. Neither shalt thou swear by thy head, for thou canst not make one hair white or black." If you understand these sayings, really you will know this is truly gospel; otherwise what does gospel mean to you? Our bodies are the momentary effect of a certain cause, our parents, and this transitory existence is like a bubble on the ocean wave. By our illusion we enjoy life and mourn death. All of these are appearing by our thought, discrimination. But there is nothing which is living or dying.

In the *Mumon-kan* (*Gateless Gate*)[13] there is an interesting koan:

When Eno,[14] the Sixth Patriarch of Zen transmission, came to a temple garden in which the flag announcing a priest's lecture was flying, two monks were arguing about the flag.
One monk said: "The wind is moving."
But the other monk said: "The flag is moving."
Each held to his own opinion and the argument would never have finished had the Sixth Patriarch not said:
"Your minds are moving; not the flag and not the wind also."

You can graduate from the problem of life-and-death[15] if you live while you are living and if you die when death comes to you. People think they were born, and therefore they will die. They are no different from the patients who are ill with eye disease and see empty sparks or flowers. It is a funny thing if someone thinks rabbits have horns or snakes have feet. But if someone realizes that there is no self existence and therefore there is no death-and-life, we call him an enlightened person, or the person who reached the other shore. A great Japanese Zenji, Shido-Bunan (died 1676) said in his stanza:

> Always having nothing to think
> Is the practice to become Buddha.
> With no thinking doing whatever is good.
> While living become a dead person.
> Die, die, die completely, and
> Do everything as you like.
> This is Nirvana.

When people don't become aware of this Law, they must hate bad circumstances and they must love good circumstances. And endlessly they must transmigrate through the six suffering worlds. If people become aware that life-and-death is like a dream, and know even a piece of hair is Buddha itself, we call that enlightenment. Getting enlightenment is like awakening from a bad dream. In the night you dream that you are wandering in a strange country and longing to go home to your native land, to your house. But in that situation you cannot go home even though you try with all your might. When you awake from the dream, however, you notice you are in your land, in your house, in your bed. Like this dream, if we awake from the delusion of death-and-life, this world itself is the other shore, Nirvana.

If I talk in this way someone may think I am saying that our life is empty, everything is empty. But that is not understanding my talking very well. If you are aware that our death and life are only the vision which was made by our discrimination, you have no need to fear anything, you can live very well. In Japan a great poet and Zen layman said when he was on his sickbed, "Until now I was thinking Zen teaching was for knowing how we should die. But it was not true.

Zen teaching is for knowing how we should live in any circumstance."[16] Though that should be common sense for Buddhists, so-called Buddhists sometimes think Zen or Buddhism is teaching nihilism. I hope you will not misunderstand so easily what I have just said and will not make such an excuse to turn yourself away from seeking the truth. If you don't get enlightenment by yourself, no one can give it to you. A teacher can only point out to you where the correct way is. And if you don't get enlightenment you are the one who has the most suffering and who makes others also suffer.

In order to avoid misunderstanding of Jo-ken and Dan-ken I would like to introduce another koan from the *Mumon-kan*.

> Priest Tosotsu settled the following three questions for the trainers to test their understanding. The first is: "Studying Zen by visiting various Masters is only for the purpose of becoming Buddha by seeing your nature. Then, now at this very moment where is your real nature?" The second is: "If you realize your real nature, you can be free from the world of suffering, death-and-life. When the light of your eyes is failing how can you be free from death-and-life?" Third: "If you have freed yourself from suffering, from death-and-life, you should know where you are going. Then where are we going when the elements of our body separate?"

The editor of this book kindly gave a commentary on this koan for us: "If you can answer these three questions, you can be master wherever you are and in any situation you will live as truth itself. But if you are not yet ready to answer, please digest these foods very well and know that chewing badly soon makes you hungry while chewing well keeps you long satisfied."

Next, about *shin-gyo*. *Shin* means the essence or most important thing, the core. The Hannya Sutra is the essence not only of the six hundred volumes of the Mahaprajnaparamita Sutra but of all Mahayana Buddhist sutras. The mind which is essence surely has its great work. But even if you seek its formal existence, there is not;

therefore we call it shin. It is just like an onion. Even if you try to find the essence of the onion by peeling one piece after another, finally you will find nothing in your hand.

Gyō comes from *kyō*. For making the idiom shin-gyo, kyo changed to gyo euphonically. Kyo means sutra. In Sanskrit sutra originally meant "warp." When we make cloth or a rosary, if there are no warp threads, all the weft threads or beads will be confused. Therefore sutra, as warp, is for solving the confusion of the world. In China all the sayings of saints such as Confucius or Lao-tse were respectfully called kyo, with the meaning of "eternal and unchanging." That is why when translators wrote down the sayings of the Indian saint, Sakyamuni Buddha, they chose kyo for sutra. Anyway, sutra actually means "Law" or "Eternity." Sutra means the Buddha-nature exists always, regardless of the phenomenon of life-and-death from the beginningless beginning to the endless end of the world. All sentient beings have this Buddha-nature, sutra, in their lives. Therefore, in this respect, letters are not sutra, words are not sutra, but our formless mind is sutra. When we see a mountain, why doesn't the mountain protect itself from being seen? When we see a river, why doesn't the river protect itself from being seen? And in case you cannot see them, who is interfering with seeing them? Here there is a Chinese poem by So-toba:

> The whispers of mountain stream are so eloquent.
> Since last night they made eighty-four thousand stanzas.
> There are no mountains which are not pure Dharma.
> How can I tell to others when I meet with them?

This poem is telling that there is sutra everywhere, but to see it depends on our eyes and to hear it depends on our ears. Therefore since old times many people were enlightened by seeing the color or by hearing the sound: Sakyamuni Buddha by seeing the morning star, Reiun by seeing the peach blossoms, Kyogen by hearing the hitting sound of a stone among the dust he threw into the bamboo grove when he was cleaning the garden. My Zen Master, Itsugai, who is

一擊忘所智
更不假修治

西曆一九七三年十二月
星漢かく

presently the Abbot of Myo-shin-ji, told me his experience one night when I was in agony because I could not solve any koan.

Well, when you are in desperation, you are standing next door to enlightenment. 'A cornered rat will bite the cat' was said for such a case. When I was in Daitoku Monastery all the monks of that year were able to see their original nature and they could not suppress showing their enjoyment on all occasions. But I, unable to see my original nature, could not pass any koan.

Then I vowed to meditate for one hundred days in the graveyard after all the monks went to bed. It was in the cold of winter. From Mt. Hiei, mountain blasts visited and blew icy snow on my shoulders, head and legs, over all of my body every night. I did not move from my seat even to relieve myself. At the beginning my under robe was very warm but soon it became icily cold.

I bet all my body and mind to solve the koan. When I went to my teacher's room to show my understanding, I felt I was dying and fainted before finishing my saying. It happened so often because my physical energy was weakened and because of the extreme contrast of temperature from the graveyard to my teacher's room. I tried to become the koan itself because that is the only way to understand koans. I tried, but I could not and one hundred days passed away. I seemed not to be a living person in this world, with my desperation, the exhaustion of my energy, and, I must add, my strenuous efforts to get enlightenment.

There came a rest day—indeed there is no rest day in the monastery but lazy monks use 'taking care of the body day' as rest day. All the monks however went to the town for their relaxation. I had not such leisure, but I spared one hour to visit a shrine at which my mother was all the time having worship during her life. Then I also had worship and prayed for enlightenment. And I had meditation.

Evening came but the monks had not come back yet. Their clothes were blowing in the evening air. I took and folded them and put them in front of the monks' rooms. And I thought, they will come back with the tiredness of a day's play. So I prepared the bath for them. It was a large bath tub for many people, as you know. I put a lot of firewood into the furnace. And before I knew, I was entering into sanmai. There must have been a great smoke in the furnace without any burning. And still I was putting firewood into the furnace unconsciously. All of a sudden a stream of red fire came out and hit my whole body. That moment was when I could see my original nature and my koan was really a laughable, reasonable thing. It was not strange, not a paradoxical thing at all. I was dancing, singing with enjoyment.

Zen Master Itsugai's story tells that his eyes, his ears, and the fire as well were sutra. What sutra is depends on us. Because whatever we call it, we all have Buddha-nature. If you understand this truth, reading the sutra is like walking in your mind. Not only this sutra; whatever you face is just your mind itself.

III The Bodhisattva Way

When the Bodhisattva Avalokitesvara practiced the deep Prajna-paramita,

Kan ji zai bo sa, gyo jin han nya ha ra mi ta ji,

Sutras are usually in three parts. The introduction tells the origin of the sutra and in what connection it was preached. The center is the main subject of the sutra. And the conclusion tells how we should teach the sutra in the future. This Hannya-shin-gyo, however, is only the main subject part, because this sutra is the essence of all Buddhist sutras, and conciseness was intended. Historically Hannya-shin-gyo was preached by Sakyamuni Buddha when he was between fifty and seventy years old, which was at least twenty years after his attaining Buddhahood under the Bodhi tree, that being, according to tradition, the morning of December eighth.

Sakyamuni Buddha was born on April eighth, 463 B.C. When he was twenty-nine years old he entered into the priesthood and after six years of hard training, he attained his Buddhahood. On February fifteenth, 383 B.C. he entered into Nirvana physically also (in the English expression, passed away). This year of 1972 is already the 2355th year after Sakyamuni Buddha's death.

Now let me talk about the *Bodhisattva* Avalokitesvara. Since Avalokitesvara is one of the Bodhisattvas, at first I will explain Bodhisattva. *Bodhi* means "wisdom" or "enlightenment." *Sattva* means "sentient being." Thus Bodhisattva means literally "enlightened person." A Bodhisattva "seeks the Buddhahood above and helps all sentient beings below." In other words, he seeks the great wisdom and the great mercy which were perfected by Sakyamuni Buddha. Today people will feel some strangeness as if entering into a vacuum when they hear of living with mercy for all sentient beings. "Mercy" *(Jihi)* means "giving the enjoyment to others and getting the suffering of others." Most people nowadays request their rights. Among Buddha's teachings there is the teaching of carrying out one's duty, but there is not the teaching of insisting on one's rights. I don't like the fashion of the revolution of women's or students' power. Not because they are women or students, but because they are too sincere about only requesting their rights. At least Buddhists should live for others even if they need to have two meals instead of three. For that, cut off the ego and live as a Bodhisattva. And if we live as Bodhisattvas, we will know really "there is enough dress and food in the Bodhisattva Way, but there is no Bodhisattva in the dress and food."

Every man has the Bodhisattva mind. Only awareness is necessary, and continuing to live as a Bodhisattva. Indeed there are people who work only for money, live only by money, and die only for money. Sorrowfully, they do not know that they themselves are such respectable beings who can enjoy their lives, and can make this world Heaven from Hell.

Anyway we are all originally Buddhas, and if you believe this fact you should train until it is no longer necessary to add the word "originally." This adverb "originally" is one condition for us. "If we testify by the Bodhisattva training, we are Buddhas" clearly expresses this condition.

Then now you may want to know more about the training of the Bodhisattva. Hannya-haramita, about which I already talked, is one of the virtuous conducts of the training of Bodhisattvas. Always Bodhisattvas practice the six kinds of paramitas (*sat pāramitah* in Sanskrit). In order to reach the other shore of Nirvana, these trainings are indispensable. For such Bodhisattvas, practicing these trainings is the only enjoyable and important thing. These are:

1. *Dāna-pāramitā*—donation
2. *Śila-pāramitā*—keeping the precepts
3. *Ksanti-pāramitā*—perseverance
4. *Virya-pāramitā*—assiduity
5. *Dhyāna-pāramitā*—meditation
6. *Prajñā-pāramitā*—wisdom

The first paramita, Dana is "donation" in English. There are three kinds of donation: the donation of materials, the donation of the Law, and the donation of "non-afraidness."[1] The donation of materials means to give gold, silver or such treasures, money, clothes, labor, and so on. Usually laymen are the hosts of this kind of donation to the church or temple.

The second donation, of the Law, means teaching the truth of Buddha-Law by good expedients in order to lead people to the enlightened world. Therefore, priests are hosts of the donation of the Law to the layman.

Zen Master Itsugai taught to me over and over again that a donation must be performed with three purities: the purity of the host of the donation, the purity of the receiver, and the purity of the things donated. And he said, "Don't receive any donation if the host is an impure person, don't receive any donation if you the receiver are impure, don't receive any donation if the donated things are impure. The same applies when you are the host of the donation." And he added, "When these three purities are prepared very well, you should ask the donation at first from your family. If they don't give to you, other people cannot see any reason to give to you. After that you should visit the poorest family in your village or town. They may refuse to give to you, but you must try to succeed to get from them even a cent. If they offer their best donation, others can see enough reason that they should offer you their best."

The world is becoming so cold by the incorrect usage of science. Without religious mind, science is only a cold devil. By the lack of religious mind sentient beings are losing their place to live in this world and insentient beings are taking over our place. There are many roads for automobiles, but not so many for human beings anymore. Under such conditions human beings will see each other only as matter. If they agree among themselves that they are human beings, they must fight to secure their place. But they cannot fight so much. Then they must deny seeing each other as human beings. If you observe animals in the forest, you can understand how important their chosen places are for them. But for human beings to fight each other like animals is not the correct way, and to deny seeing each other as human beings is also not the correct way. Incorrect usage of science, the lacking of religious mind, is the real reason for this cold modern world. Therefore, especially under such conditions we should realize the importance of religion, and if we practice even these donations only, this world will become Heaven.

When we judge the greatness of a country what is our compass? When I was staying in Thailand as a training monk, I wondered about the standard to judge the greatness of a country. It is evidently not weapon power. No one can kill our recognition of our dying even though someone can kill our physical body. Even if the Third World War occurs and as many atomic bombs as the eggs of a frog explode, still no one can attack my mind. I will feel pain and cry and lament, but I know who is in pain, who is crying, who is lamenting. Our mind is really an inviolable thing. And even though I must die, still *I* am dying, and if I die I live the life of death. No one can destroy the life of this world. Since weapon power cannot be considered for judging the greatness of a country at all, what is the standard? Money? If you read my above sentences, it also cannot be. Money is only material, which cannot move by itself. Calling a country economically great is giving a rich name to the country which is living in illusion. Even a cat can understand such a thing. If you give money to a cat, he will merely yawn. But if you use your mind a little and buy some suitable food to give to him, you will see how he will become your good friend. Some people think quite sincerely that the greatness of a country depends on the number of beautiful women in that country. I guess that is why there are beauty contests. But in my opinion all women have their own beauty. Still if someone estimates the value of a certain type of beautiful woman, I should say he is being unfair to all other women by his ego, which is illusion. Sorrowfully, he is making a narrow and ugly world since there are not so many of his illusory type of beautiful women. When we think that the culture of a country is the standard for judging its greatness we are making the same kind of mistake as the Miss America contest. The reasons are the same.

While thinking these things in Thailand I was a religious mendicant. In the early morning while haze was rising from the river and green fields and from narrow street after narrow street, I was walking with the bowl to receive quietly the offered rice. Here and there in the mist we who were trainers could see each other in yellow robes, bowls hanging from our shoulders, our feet bare. At the corners of streets or in front of houses laymen were awaiting our coming by putting many kinds of food on stands. Sometimes I could see a laywoman awaiting my coming on the river bank because she came by her boat from a far village. Usually I could get enough food for breakfast and lunch. They gave me bananas, mangos, rice, oranges, pineapple, coconut, and many fruits unknown to me, and also lotus flowers to encourage our training. Every morning I did this. But one day I was told by a Thai friend that all these laymen don't eat their breakfast unless they have offered their food to the priests. I was so surprised by hearing this saying that I stood up in the middle of the street straight as a broom. My friend continued his saying, "Furthermore, they are not eating such good food as they give to us. They are too poor to satisfy both themselves and others." Momentarily on my brow my mother's eyes appeared smiling. And when I noticed myself, I could not stop the tears which were falling on my bare feet. I don't like to describe more than this about my experience.

Later I came to know still more about Thailand people. My friend's saying was perfectly correct. Ninety percent of Thailand's population are practicing such donation every morning. Doing this practice is the one most enjoyable thing for them. They will not expect any thanks from the priest because in their saying, "Giving to others, especially to the trainers of Buddhahood, is the most enjoyable matter for us. If by giving we can become a better, purer person, is that not a happy matter? I hope in my next life I can become a priest though by the Great Law of Cause and Effect I could not become one in this world. I know practicing the Buddhist life all day, all our life with all of our power is the greatest happiness. You are my superior."

I think the greatness of a country must be judged by the religious mind and practice of its people.

Now I have talked about two kinds of donation, of material and of the Law. For the donation of the Law, I can simply add that we must really love people and should use any kind of method for making a person happy, and we must have patience. The teacher of the Law, the priest, must be mother and father for the laymen regardless of age or sex. Teaching the Law is like growing plants. We should not force them to grow up in a certain way except that they should grow up as plants to give shade to thirsty travellers. Even if we impatiently pull a plant to make it grow quickly, it will only be destroyed. The teacher of the Law does not intend to teach anything; he only makes the laymen awaken for their Buddhahood. Well, the teacher of the Law must know this enough if he is teacher of the Law; therefore I have no need to talk about this anymore. However I must tell how we should find the real teacher, though I am talking about that already. Please find a Bodhisattva.

Next, the donation of non-afraidness means at the risk of one's own life to save others from disaster or misfortune. In the Preface I introduced a story that is a good example. It is indeed one of the most difficult acts for human beings. It seems to me that people who at the risk of their own lives ensnare others into disaster or misfortune are more numerous than people who save others from these situations at the risk of their own lives. But most mothers will save at least their own children. And in this world, still there are a few good examples. My life was saved in such a disaster by an American girl who became my wife. The person who knows it knows.

Modern mass-communication media wouldn't make so much news if human conduct were good. In general reporters are like vultures who eat only carrion. Though they have their proper place, they should report more good news as well. Or are they knowing "the sound of an alcohol flask"? If there is no sound when you are shaking an alcohol flask, that flask is empty or full. If there is a sound, "chap-chap," that flask is almost empty. To resume, it is a difficult thing to save another life at the risk of our own life. But everyone has the ability, only it is covered by our egoistic illusion. If you see your own original nature, such a way to live is common sense; it is no more difficult than walking in your own garden. At first people must recognize the difficulty of such conduct, must recognize their own original capability. And then they should train to polish their ability until it becomes an easy matter. And continue to live the practical life of Bodhisattvas.

The second paramita, Sila, is keeping the precepts. This includes all social orders or laws, and Buddhist moralities. In Buddha's Law all social laws are included, but all social laws cannot always include the Buddha's Law. This is so because some social laws were made by the ego of a particular country or society for a particular time. There is no better way than studying the Buddha Law at first. Buddhism is the teaching to become Buddha. Therefore Buddhists need the precepts even for their own sakes. For Buddhists there is no case that because no one is seeing us we can do bad things. Even in the room with closed doors, a Buddhist should know, "Heaven knows, earth knows, the wall knows, self knows. . . ." If Buddhists need precepts for themselves as individuals, how much more need there is in the life of human groups. We human beings cannot live alone. If we don't keep the precepts strongly to help each other, we cannot live, and the Bodhisattva Way will become a dream. Then for a Bodhisattva, keeping precepts is necessary by all means.

There are two kinds of precepts, which differ according to how we keep them. One kind we are forced from the outside to keep. The other we keep with enjoyment for our own Bodhisattva life. When we were born we were purely Law itself, but somehow we became separated from the Law. That is why we should force ourselves to keep many precepts and should keep them until the forcing power disappears and we get the situation in which we can live as we like without living illegally. The common process of sincere trainers is first to keep the teacher's precepts, then to separate from the teacher to make one's own precepts, and finally to go beyond the teacher's precepts.

Though I trained in a Japanese Zen monastery and have lived as a Buddhist priest almost ten years I wonder about the practice of Buddhist precepts in Japan. In fact when I arrived in Thailand, one Thai priest said to me about the practice of Buddhist precepts and priests in Japan, "We cannot accept a Japanese priest as a Buddhist priest. Because Japanese priests don't practice the precepts." Then it was necessary for me to receive the ordination rites in order to train as a Thailand priest.

Certainly Japanese Buddhism is contributing a lot of things to Japanese culture and life. Especially Buddhist philosophy progressed and was studied very well. But without practice, Buddhism has no more life than a philosophical mummy. It is evidently not the way of Buddhism to have luxurious dress while calling it a robe, to drink alcohol saying it is "Hannya water." Not only these small matters, but seeking fame, rank, money in the daytime and indulging in passion in the night. This is very far from being a Buddhist layman and certainly not the face of a priest at all. It is a devil with a human body. I don't like to stimulate the curiosity for scandal while there are good people; but Buddhists feel sensitive shame when mud is given to the face of Buddha.

In practicing the precepts, there are many difficult problems, such as what are the real precepts for Buddhists. The marriage of priests, or the eating of meat are examples of such questions.

About these two, Zen Master Itsugai talked furiously: "I wish I were the Prime Minister of Japan. If I were, I could deprive priests who are marrying and eating fish and meat of their false priesthood. If the priest marries, he must hold his wife with his right hand and he must hold his child with his left hand. In such a time, with which hand can he hold the people, all sentient beings?" And while glaring at all of us who were his disciples, he continued,

Eating fish or meat is studying the way to become beasts. Can't you see blood spilling from the mouth of such a priest? Can't you hear the grief of innumerable animals which were killed? In the night under the yellow moon a dog is bellowing ceaselessly on the cliff facing the dark valley and on the roof a black cat is standing its long tail. Why are they doing so? The holy priest Myoe (died 1232) was so merciful he left a poem:

> How pitiful to hear
> The sound of crying mosquitoes.
> It reminds me that
> I shared my blood once upon a time.

And about Priest Myoe there are many good stories. This is one of them:

One day in the snowy morning a deer wandered into his temple garden. As soon as Priest Myoe saw the deer he picked up a stick to chase it out, shouting, "Go out, go, go!"

The deer ran away beyond the garden house. The disciples of Priest Myoe, however, were watching this sight and they complained,

"Our teacher, why should you chase the deer out? He was sorrowfully cold and hungry on the mountain so he came to the village to find food."

Priest Myoe replied, "I know about it as well as you. But in this village there are many hunters with bow and arrow. I hope he can escape from these hunters and patiently await the coming of spring."

After talking, Zen Master Itsugai clasped his hands for having worship and finished his lecture to us. So often I remembered his talking, especially when I sat down quietly in the dark room. When I was in the monastery I was a young boy and I had much difficulty understanding why we should not marry and should not eat meat or fish. For me it seemed unnatural as a human being to keep such precepts. But without a real solution, I could not be satisfied either way, to keep or not, though formally on the surface I kept such precepts. After staying a few years in the monastery and by solving many koans related to the precepts, I could solve my confusion. But I wanted to make completely sure of my understanding of the precepts. Therefore I went to Thailand. By keeping more than two hundred and fifty Buddhist moralities, I almost reached my satisfaction about understanding those which I would like to introduce to you here.

At first there is "The Teaching of the Seven Buddhas":

> Don't do anything bad,
> Please do everything good,
> And keep mind pure.
> This is the teaching of all Buddhas.

The third phrase, "And keep mind pure," means we are originally pure; everyone has Buddha nature. Though we think all good and bad are existing, in fact they are conditional forms which were harmonized by Cause and Effect in time and by mutual relations in space. There is not any ultimate, settled existence. Therefore we can be pure. If we are not pure at the beginning, it is unnatural to desire to keep pure. Then this third phrase shows the original reason for the first two phrases. When we practice the first two phrases we will see that together they have the same weight as the third phrase. The last phrase unifies all three preceding phrases, saying make your mind empty and keep the precepts by which all of the important matters of life will be done. If someone asks me, "What is bad and good?" without realizing that he is already knowing by himself, I will say, "It was said in a sutra that letting your mind follow the Dharma, Law, is called 'good', but opposing it is called 'bad'." And in another sutra it was said that "Giving enjoyment and profit to yourself and others is good conduct." In any case, good and bad are depending on how you will use everything in each situation. Even God, if used by a person for protecting his ego, will become a devil; even a devil, if used by a person for encouraging his Buddha nature, will become God.

Next I should show Buddhist confession. Because without confession, no one can keep the precepts.

> The Sentences of Confession
> All the evil karma ever committed by me since of old,
> On account of greed, anger, and folly, which have no beginning,
> Born of my body, mouth, and thought—
> I now make full open confession of it.[2]

I hope you can accept this confession as you read. Karma came from the Sanskrit *karman*. The original meaning is "action," but later it joined with the meaning of "cause and effect." Karma was thought of as a power which is working continuously since the beginning of the universe. If there is an ex-convict who has become aware of the happiness of living correctly, very often he will not be welcomed in the social world even though he lives a correct life. Though it is a very sorrowful situation, he is influenced by the power created by his former action and by many causes and effects surrounding him. When he sees this karma he can have real confession and can live a satisfied life instead of complaining about his unwelcomed situation. Not only an ex-convict but we human beings all should recognize our karma. And when we think of karma we will not think that it was made by others but by ourselves, "by me." Buddhists have no Adam and Eve; always, if it is evil karma, it was made "by me." When we think in this way, the thought of karma becomes very active, subjective, a rather bright posture for living, instead of passive, fatalistic or darkly pessimistic. Really this "by me" is the secret energy to order oneself to come up from darkness into light, from a regrettable life to the creative, moral world.[3]

Buddhists count three basic evils of human desire: greed, anger, and folly. These are summarizing the lack of wisdom, of Hannya. If we confess, naturally we are already entering into the Buddhist belief, which means having faith for the Three Treasures of Buddhism: Buddha, Dharma, and *Sangha*. Buddha is the one awakened to the truth, the one who is Sakyamuni Buddha. Dharma is the law which is attained by Buddha and is taught. Sangha is the trainers who are practicing the Law. For Buddhists therefore there are "The Precepts for Believing the Three Treasures" (*San-Ki-Kai*):

I believe the Buddha with full respect,
I believe the Dharma with full respect,
I believe the Sangha with full respect;
To the Buddha, the incomparably honored one,
To the Dharma, honorable for its purity,
To the Sangha, honorable for its harmonious life;
I believe the Buddha completely,
I believe the Dharma completely,
I believe the Sangha completely.

Without belief we cannot live the Bodhisattva life. All lives of the social world will die, all enjoyments of the social world will be exhausted sooner or later. But the Three Treasures will not die, will not be exhausted. They are innumerable, inexhaustible and immeasurable.

Now I shall talk of the ten important Buddhist precepts. Though I say it tediously, all of these are meaningless without practice, valueless, just like the saying, pearls before swine. I am hoping people will practice as much as they can. Therefore I will not engage in heated discourse, but only speak of the practical understanding by my life. Please don't be as the proverb says, "a mere scholar, a mere ass."

The ten important precepts are as follows: I. Not to kill; II. Not to steal; III. Not to commit adultery; IV. Not to lie; V. Not to drink alcohol; VI. Not to slander; VII. Not to insult; VIII. Not to covet; IX. Not to anger; X. Not to slander the Three Treasures.

I. Not to kill means to help the lives. To make alive we must kill that which we call ego. Kill all and make alive all is the ideal practice of this precept. You can eat meat or fish just as you eat vegetables, but do not forget to make them come alive through your active Bodhisattva life.

II. Not to steal means to give to others. If you don't practice donation you are stealing. In old Japan there was a thief who entered into jail to teach the Law to the prisoners. The thief was a priest.

III. Not to commit adultery means to have sex correctly. There is no such law that one cannot have sex because he is a priest, or that he can have because he is a layman. Priest and layman are simple names for the phenomena. All human beings should live as Bodhisattvas whatever their age, sex, wealth, whether priest or layman, regardless of all contrastable social phenomena. No one can have sex or marry if he cannot live as a Bodhisattva by such conduct. At least the person who has sex must consider in addition to his own happiness that of his companion and of the third person who will be most affected by his act. If these three concerned people can be satisfied, then sex or marriage is the natural Law of human beings. And that will be worthy of being called free sex. I think such a blessed married family, father and mother and child taking the bath together is the most happy, most beautiful scene on this earth.

We must know surely that adultery is the enemy of love. Having sex without marriage destroys the building of love. When we marry there is the bud of love which is small, weak and quiet. By the married life we must grow that bud of love and make great, strong and dynamic, creative love. When you change your companion, the bud of love is cut off and again you must start from the beginning to build the love for growing the love. Know that love is a living creature which cannot be gotten by being picked up like a stone. Without taking care ceaselessly with the love to the love, you cannot get any love while you are in this world. It is said that if a female crane becomes pregnant by adultery, she will be bitten to death by all of the males of her group. Know by yourself that real love comes from fidelity. Don't burn out your respectable pure love by the fire of passion.

IV. Not to lie. This must be kept for oneself and for others. The most miserable lie is *māna* which is pride. Since old times, in the

Abhidharma-vijnaptimatrata Sect of Buddhism mana was divided into seven kinds. First is the simple pride of thinking oneself better than a worse person and of the same worth as an equal. The second is more than simple pride: it is to think of oneself as better than an equal and to think of one who is better than oneself as one's equal. The third is much too much pride: to think of oneself as better than a better person. Fourth is a kind of ignorance of self-existence, which means that one thinks his body or mind is an eternal being, unchangeable. Fifth may be called pride reaching the extreme, when one thinks he has gotten enlightenment though he has not. Sixth is a humble pride, when one thinks he is only a little worse than a better person. Seventh is an evil pride which is to think one has virtue in spite of the fact that he has not. This last is the most miserable lie, I think. We need to say to ourselves, "Know thyself." With the help of many such sayings by great persons, I too have been trying since childhood to mend my self-hating character which has pride in this way and that. I am practicing by writing a diary every night to reflect myself these past fourteen years. I am trying to see my mind whenever I face the mirror, not only my face. Anyway, seeing ourselves with others' eyes is a difficult thing, but we will try.

V. Not to drink alcohol. This can include other intoxicants which deny our healthy works of body and mind. That is nihilism. Therefore this precept means do not be drunken by any kind of thing which poisons our health. I have heard that Sakyamuni Buddha allowed a disciple, Gida, to drink alcohol because he could not preach in front of the people without it. Though I don't know this to be a historical fact, I think it is a splendid matter if one can really do a good thing by the help of alcohol. In the limited sense of a Japanese proverb, "Alcohol is best among one hundred medicines," drinking it is not bad at all.

VI. Not to slander. The slanderer is slandering himself after all. The enjoyment of others' misfortune comes from the same psychology as slandering.

VII. Not to insult. This precept will be destroyed by the mind which admires only oneself. My mother used to scold me even when I complained about the bad weather. All of the universe is oneself.

VIII. Not to covet. Coveting means wanting to get more than necessity and not giving to others who are more in need than oneself. We should know "to know enough." Otherwise the thankful life will not present itself for us. Of giving there is no end while there are so many others; giving to a Bodhisattva is better than giving to a thousand ghosts.

IX. Not to anger means train very well in the Bodhisattva Way. If you are sincerely seeking Buddhahood, you have no time to anger over small social phenomena. All social phenomena, either public or private, are good chances to train. To anger and to scold must be distinguished one from the other. Scolding is the mercy of a Bodhisattva. If parents don't scold children, children aren't receiving the love of parents, as can so often be observed. To anger makes long regret even though anger is only for a moment. If we are training, however, all anger from others to us becomes the merciful teaching and all anger from us to others also. Anyway, please don't anger; train in the Bodhisattva Way.

X. Not to slander the Three Treasures means to know that we ourselves are the Three Treasures; without the Three Treasures we ourselves could not be.

Until now I have been talking about Sila-paramita. The important thing is that without real confession we cannot keep any precepts. Because real confession is to regret all evils which were done in past time, and at the same time to vow to do all good conducts. And the more important thing is knowing that the evils are in social phenomena and that in truth there are no evils anywhere. If we don't know both phenomena and Law, which are two faces of the same thing, we will not get any satisfaction for living. In this connection, please study the following two koans from a Zen textbook. One is:

Once upon a time a great Chinese poet, Haku-raku-ten, asked to Zenji Dorin, "What is the most important thing in Buddhism?"

The teacher answered, "Don't do anything bad, please do everything good."

"There are such words in Confucianism also. They will be said even by a three year old baby," said Haku-raku-ten.

"Though even a three year old baby is able to say so, even an eighty year old man can hardly practice it," Zenji Dorin replied.

This was the origin of the great poet's decision to become a Buddhist layman from a Confucianist.

Another story reads:

The Thirtieth Patriarch in Chinese Zen transmission, Kanchi, was studying under the Twenty-ninth Patriarch and asked,

"Your disciple has gotten palsy. It must be because the teacher requested, and following that the monk Kanchi answered,

"Even though I have looked for my sin, it is impossible to get it."

The teacher said, "Good, I have finished purifying your sin for you. Please live well in the Buddha, Dharma, and Sangha."

The Thirtieth Patriarch was awakened for the Law and showed his understanding to his teacher with a stanza:

> Today was the first day I knew,
> Sin is not inside,
> Not outside, and also not in between.
> Our mind is also like this,
> Buddha Law is also not two.

The third paramita, Ksanti, is perseverance. As you know, this world is filled with sufferings. Sakyamuni Buddha counted four basic sufferings: birth, old age, illness, and death. And later four other sufferings were also added as basic sufferings: those which come by separation from loved ones, meeting hated ones, being unable to get what one wants, and by one's body, sensation, thought, volition, and consciousness. By the way, in the *Madhyamāgama Sutra* Sakyamuni Buddha reflected on his youth and said to training monks the following which I will translate from a Chinese textbook:

I was very comfortable, incomparably comfortable, extremely comfortable. In my father's mansion there was a pond with lotus flowers. There in one place blue lotus flowers were planted, in another place red lotus flowers, and in still another place white lotus flowers were planted and all of this was done only for my sake. I had never used incense except from bead trees, made in Benares. So as not to touch directly with the cold, heat, dust, grass and dew, a white parasol was supported for my sake in the day and night. For such as I there were three palaces. One was for the winter, another was for the summer, and one more was for the rainy season. Then during the time of the four month rainy season, I was surrounded with dance and music played only by women in the suitable palace for the rainy season and I never went out from the palace at all. Whereas in other nations slaves, servants, and employees were offered sour gruel, in my father's mansion slaves, servants and employees were offered meals of rice and meat.

I had such rich circumstances and I was extremely comfortable, but the following thought arose for me: ignorant ordinary men are losing themselves in thought, worrying, and feeling humiliation and hatred from seeing senile men, though they themselves will get old age: it is inevitable. I am also one who will get old age: it is inevitable. I am the one who will get old age, and it is as inevitable for me as for them. But by seeing other senile ones I may worry, feel shame and hate, which is not like me. When I observed like this, my young man's spirit at youth disappeared entirely.

Ignorant ordinary men are losing themselves in thought, worrying, feeling humiliation and hatred from seeing suffering ones, though they themselves will get illness: it is inevitable. I am also one who will suffer from illness: it is inevitable. I am one who will suffer from illness and it is as inevitable for me as for them. But by seeing other suffering ones I may worry, feel shame and hate, which is not like me. When I observed like this, my healthy spirit at healthy time disappeared entirely.

Ignorant ordinary men are losing themselves in thought, worrying, feeling humiliation and hatred from seeing the dead though they themselves will die: it is inevitable. I am also one who will die: it is inevitable. I am one who will die and it is as inevitable for me as for them. But by seeing other dead ones I may worry, feel shame and hate, which is not like me. When I observed like this, my living spirit at life disappeared entirely.

With such observation of sufferings, Sakyamuni Buddha entered into the training life as a Bodhisattva. We are also Bodhisattvas. Therefore we should persevere in any circumstances, thinking whatever comes to us is a good occasion to train. The Japanese Zen monastery is one of the most sincere and hard places in which to live. Among many monasteries these three, Bairin in southern Japan, Myoshin in Kyoto, and Shogen in middle Japan are so famous for hardship that since old times they have been called the training place of devils. Other monasteries are commonly called the training place of princesses in comparison with those three. That is one reason why I chose to enter into the hardest monastery which was Shogen-ji in Gifu Prefecture. Of course, hardship depends on the personal sincerity of training, but while we are not perfectly enlightened, circumstance has great importance.

Indeed, Shogen was quite a—hard place. We needed to get up at three-thirty and could go to bed at ten in the night. When I went to bed at such a time, a command monk awakened me and said, "How can you sleep without solving any koan? Go to the mountain to meditate." Always meditation was required with cross-legged form and even when a thousand mosquitoes attacked us we could not move, or even when we fainted from pain in our legs we could not move. Even in the middle of snowy winter we meditated with windows opened wide. Food was watery gruel which clearly reflected the ceiling. Work in the daytime was on the mountain cutting wood or planting trees and in the field farming most of the time by hand. I was scolded all the time with the command, "Become the object itself!" Pilgrimage to collect money and rice was made at almost running speed, a distance of four or five hours one way from the far mountain to the town. In the snow no one was allowed to have socks. Our only shoes were straw sandals. And in my memory, usually I was beaten more than one hundred and thirty times a day by a wooden stick for the kindness, but quite often by the unkindness of senior

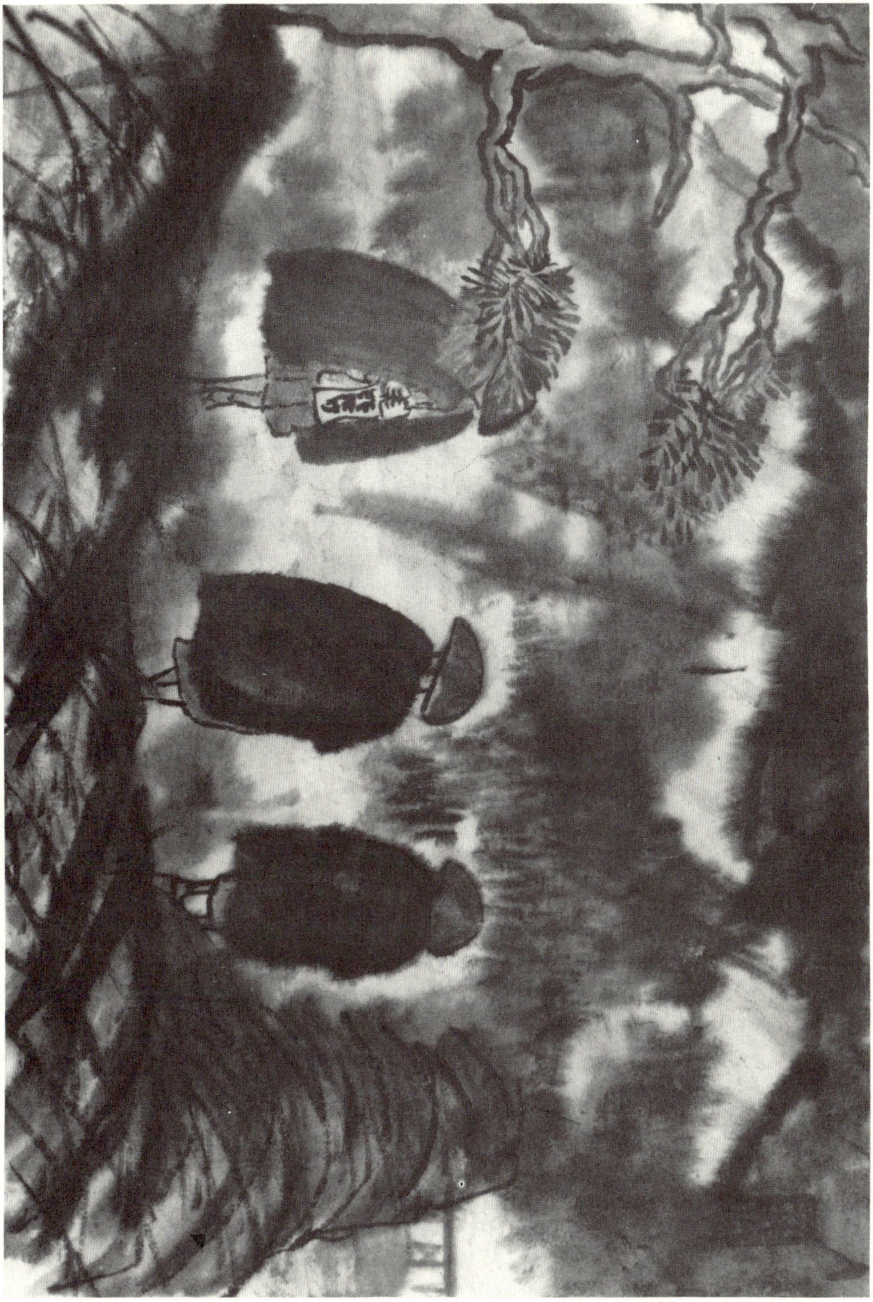

monks. Anyway, even professional soldiers could not persevere to train in this Shogen Monastery though Japan at one time had fierce soldiers, called Kamikaze.[4] Under these conditions, if we don't feel that the suffering of not solving koans is about one thousand times larger than these physical sufferings, finally we cannot solve even one koan. Many trainers escaped from this monastery without solving any koans. They did not have perseverance. If we don't have the enjoyment to live as a Bodhisattva, we cannot have perseverance. Because if we can persevere, it is not perseverance. Persevering for unperseverable matters is the real perseverance. Without Bodhisattva mind, even if someone solves one or two or even a hundred or two hundred and fifty koans, which are almost all of the koans formally required to be solved, he cannot get any real koan in real life. Such an unreal person will say empty things such as "Roshi," "Enlightenment," "Inka-shomei." These were only formal titles which are imitations of the social world by blind Zen Masters. These titles mean only that they need more and more training, more than anyone else. It is a sorrowful thing for me that in Japan, which means in the world, there are only thirty or so Zen Masters now and some of these are having only title and are not real Bodhisattvas. But for me it is enjoyable that in America, or maybe in other countries also, I can see real Bodhisattvas beginning to train without being deceived by formal titles or by any kind of mask, though most American trainers of Zen are simply not more than ghosts.

When I entered into Shogen Monastery I was fortunately surprised by that easy life. While many monks were crying from the hardship and trying to escape somehow, I found that I had had a little more suffering than the monastery since I was a baby. In my mother's talking to me, she had eaten almost nothing for a week before I was born. Even though she had gone longer than her full term, still I could not come out. In terrible pain, she crawled from her bed to the window hoping someone might see her and come to help. When she reached the window, it was a very snowy sight, I half came out. And she almost fainted. Fortunately a village midwife happened to walk past the window. My mother could hear as if in the dream world the midwife shouting toward the village, "Please, someone bring any kind of food! Anything, even dog food or cow food!" It was the middle of my mother's suffering life but for me it was the beginning.

She decided to kill me and she put me into an oven and shut it tightly. As the final decision after her thousand hesitations, she decided not to give me any more sufferings in this world. But miraculously I pushed off the tight top and came out. Then she recognized, "Someone will live even though we try to kill and someone will die even though we try to make live. Helping nature is the best thing to do."

This kind of sight was often seen in Japan after the Second World War, though Japan now worries about choosing which nickname is good for itself, "economical animal" or "political animal" or "cultural animal." At first if we don't recognize we are human beings we cannot train as Bodhisattvas and of course cannot attain Buddhahood even if we make an anti-atomic bomb or a vehicle quicker than light.

In any case, my mother got heavy illness and three important doctors said it was impossible to mend, she must die. She lived in the hospital long years. My father was a priest and half crazy and an alcoholic and he always fought with his laymen. He fought with my mother and my mother fought with my father's mother all the time. I was a floating leaf on the whirlpool of various fightings. I so often hunted food in the graveyard. Thanks to Japanese folk tradition, people offered food to the dead! My oldest brother had a brilliant brain and discovered many ways to steal skillfully. He tried to dig a tunnel to the graveyard from the house because his targets were not only of my animal step. And he freely stole electric power from the public wire. In this way he added a lot of complication to the adult's fighting by bringing the police to our home which was a temple. My second eldest brother began to become crazy and was caught by the police to be put into a hospital.

My mother, however, devoted herself to belief in the Bodhisattva Avalokitesvara of whom I will talk a little later. Her incurable disease was mended and my oldest brother was employed by a nylon company as a staff member to study synthetic fiber though he had not even gone to senior high school. And my grandmother died peacefully and most of all fightings disappeared because where there is no fire smoke also will not stand. And by the mercy of Bodhisattva Avalokitesvara my second oldest brother could mend his craziness though doctors said it would be impossible for him to mend. I fortunately was loved by both parents and by Bodhisattva Avalokitesvara and lived every day with full enjoyment. Really perseverance and Bodhisattvahood are the inside and outside of one thing. If I talk in this way about Bodhisattva Avalokitesvara you may think, how unscientifically I am talking. But at least no scientist could solve my family's problems, while a few religious people could. I think real scientists will encourage religious people through their works. I hope that through my words you could understand the necessity of having perseverance. The following experience may also be useful for you.

I was on the night train to go to the northern country. Among the passengers there was one person who saw my priest's robe and came to ask,

"Oh, my priest, please teach me about perseverance. I have done so much evil with my short impatient temper. Now my mind is just like that of a drowning man who will catch at a straw."

"If you are really sincerely asking for the perseverance I may teach you. Are you?" I replied quietly.

"With my full wish I am asking it. Please teach to me."

"It seems that you are not really asking it."

"What are you saying! I am truly seeking it. I hope you know what I have done out of my impatience, my lack of perseverance," said he and had worship to me.

"All right," I said, "after passing three more stations I will begin to preach to you."

"Why should I wait so long? Why can't you now . . . ?"

"Please wait if you would really like to know it."

From that time he kept silent and sat facing me. I was reading a book. Before I knew it, three stations had passed. He tapped my shoulder and cheerfully asked,

"We passed three stations. Can you tell to me?"

I asked, "About what?"

He was surprised and cried, "About what? Did you forget? I was asking about perseverance."

"I see. But I am in the midst of reading my book. Please wait until I finish." I began to read my book again.

He stood up and breathing rapidly with trembling hands he said, "How foolish of me! I was talking sincerely with this crazy begging priest!"

"Hey, are you angering?" I smiled to him.

"Oh, this hateful beggar. I have no time to share with you any more. I must get off at the next station, 'bye!" And he began to walk down the aisle.

I shut my book and grasped his neck and pulled him back to the seat saying, "I don't permit your getting off. In front of my eyes you have no freedom to do anything. Just sit down calmly." He feared me, obeyed and sat down. As soon as his station passed I said to him,

"Did you understand my preaching on perseverance?"

For a moment he could not understand my saying and was like a mouse crying under the rain. But suddenly sunshine, it seemed so, lighted up his face and he shouted,

"How wonderful! I experienced the perseverance! This will become my lifetime treasure!"

The fourth paramita, Virya, is assiduity, which means with effort not to do anything bad and to do everything good. There is not a thing completed without assiduity. While we are working for the money, name, power, position, and so on, it is not yet religious assiduity. But we cannot escape working for these in this society. Therefore through various social works, we should realize that we must work with effort as Bodhisattvas. That means to realize our works are not for money but for creating Nirvana on this earth. Work must be done without expecting any social rewards.

There were three tombstone dealers in an old town.

A passing philosopher asked the first dealer, "What are you doing?"

"Can't you see what I am doing? I am carving the stone," was the first stone-cutter's reply.

The philosopher went on to the next dealer and asked in the same way, "What are you doing?"

"I am making money," came the answer.

Then this philosopher visited the last dealer and asked, "What are you doing?"

"I am building a temple," he replied, carving the stone.

When I heard this story as a child, I thought it shows the essence of a great worker. Indeed we must work for making the religious world, for making Heaven on this earth. For that, assiduity not to do anything bad but to do everything good is necessary. And we should know that if we work to bring forth Nirvana, the purpose of the work is the process and the process is the purpose. Here the beautiful Bodhisattva life will appear for us. Some persons divide the purpose and the process and even though they do quite good effort they cannot get any satisfaction for their lives. And other people think the purpose and the process are one, without living as Bodhisattvas, and they fall into the ignorant life. If we live as Bodhisattvas with the purpose and the process, there is no difference between the two.

Of the Six Paramitas of Bodhisattva practices, this Virya, assiduity, is the most important. Because without assiduity no others will be accomplished. Fortunately our ancestors had great love for us and left many good examples for encouraging the practice of assiduity. Among many such examples the one which must be the best for fresh trainers is the book *Zen-kan-saku-shin, The Whips to Get Through Zen Borders,* edited by Great Teacher Unsei Renchi (or Shuko, 1535-1615 in China). I am also a person who is getting from this book ceaseless love and encouragement which are like my mother and father. Of the "Zen Borders," Great Teacher Unsei Renchi himself says in the foreword of the book,

> Why are there borders for Zen? For the Way there is no inside and no outside; therefore there is neither entering nor leaving. But

for the ways of people there is delusion and enlightenment. Then wise officers at the borders cannot avoid preventing the person who would go through secretly with strange words or dress, by opening or shutting the border gate at suitable times and carefully using the key and locking and examining strictly.

Zen is not Zen Sect's Zen. Zen should be understood as meaning the Bodhisattva life, Way. Unsei Renchi is saying that while we are not attaining Bodhisattvahood, even though we try to practice the Bodhisattva Way we cannot get beyond dualistic misunderstanding, such as thinking of delusion and enlightenment. He edited this book for practical trainers. At the end of the foreword he writes:

If you read this book, your mind to seek the Way will be encouraged, your spirit and attitude will live freshly, and impetuously but spontaneously you can advance, whipping an inferior horse. A person may say, "This book was edited for the one who is not yet going through the borders. What is the point of reading this for the one who has gone far beyond the borders already?" There are, however, more borders after the border. The person who thinks such a question is too quickly satisfied with little profits, is like the fugitive escaping from the dangerous tiger's mouth after mimicking a rooster's cry. He is the one whose pride has reached the extreme. While you are not ascertaining the source of the stream and cannot tramp all mountains, don't be anxious to celebrate the offering party for other trainers. It can be held after breaking through the last profound border and running far beyond with warning whip in hand.

"The mimicking of a rooster's cry" referred to by the editor came from an old Chinese history book, *Shiki*. In this book Mo-sho-kun assumed a false name and went to the border of Kankoku. According to orders, the gate of the border was not to be opened before the crying of the roosters. That night one of Mo-sho-kun's servants imitated the sound of a rooster so skillfully that many roosters followed his mimicking. Then the officer of the border thought morning had come and opened the gate. In this way Mo-sho-kun's group could safely get through the border.

Anyway, the editor of this book, Great Teacher Unsei Renchi, hoped strongly for us that we will really train not only on the surface, and he is encouraging us to attain Bodhisattvahood with unspeakable assiduity. Therefore I would like to introduce some of the contents of this book by my translation, hoping it can be in compliance with his wish. I will translate Part Two which is a brief description of the assiduous training of various Zen Patriarchs. *Comments* are those of the editor, and I will sometimes add a few superfluities following an asterisk.[5]

Brief Descriptions of the Assiduity of the Patriarchs

Meditating alone in a quiet room

Great Teacher Doan meditated alone in a quiet room for twelve years endeavoring with all his spiritual power and working over his conceptions. And finally he got profound enlightenment.

Comment—This old respectable teacher could get profound enlightenment by endeavoring with all his spiritual power and working over all his conceptions, but not by simple calm sitting.

*—For lazy people, twelve years seems like such a long time, but for sincere persons it is a moment. For the unrestingly turning water mill there is no ice.

Meditating in the tree on the cliff

Zenji Jorin threw off the lectures of the sutras and practiced meditation. But while he was meditating, sleepiness puzzled his mind. From a high cliff facing a valley a thousand feet deep, a tree projected. He laid grasses in the tree and sat with cross-legged posture and concentrated his mind and passed one day and night. His whole body and mind were concentrated because the fear of falling to his death was strong. By continuing in this way he got great enlightenment.

*—"Threw off the lectures of the sutras" does not mean to throw them away literally. It means to practice the things which they say. Zenji Rinzai said, "All the teachings such as the Three Vehicles and the twelve types of scripture are toilet paper." Needless to say, this means if we practice the teachings they are toilet paper which we can thankfully use to clean all of our dirt, sin. But if we don't practice, they are all no more than dirty toilet paper.

Eating the grasses and living among the trees

Zenji Tudatsu entered into Mt. Taihaku without any food. When he was hungry he ate the grasses, and when he rested he leaned on a tree. Ceaselessly he meditated and thought on the deep truth while five years passed. It happened that he hit a clod of earth with a stick. And he got enlightenment by seeing the broken clod.

Comment—Even if you eat the grasses and live among the trees, if you don't think the deep truth and if you pass many days aimlessly you are almost no different from a rustic woodcutter.

*—Entering into the forest should not be done for escaping from the social world but for creating the power to contribute to the social world.

Without undressing

Zenji Sho of Konko Temple entered into the priesthood at age thirteen and climbed Mt. Koyo at age nineteen and trained under Priest Kasho while three years passed. But he never undressed and also never lay down to sleep. When he was at Mt. Koya he stayed in the same way. And finally he got enlightenment entirely.

Piercing oneself with a gimlet

Jimyo, Kokusen, and Roya made a group to train under Funyo. It was the cold season at the east side of the Yellow River. Then many people hesitated to train there. But Jimyo had a strong wish to train in the Way and endeavored every morning and evening. During the night meditation when sleepiness came, he pierced himself with a gimlet. Later the Law was transmitted to him from Zenji Zensho at Funyo and he made the prosperity of Zen. He was admiringly called "the lion at the west side of the Yellow River."

*—Our body was given by the Buddha. Therefore we should not hurt it. But still it is better to hurt part of the body than lose the whole body.

Never slighting anything even in a dark room

Zenji Wanshi was studying at first under Shijun at Tanka. One day he discussed with the monks about a koan and laughed involuntarily. Teacher Shijun scolded, "You lost a lot of things with your one laugh. Don't you know the saying that if you are not yourself even for a moment you are equal to a dead person?" Wanshi had worship twice and kept the teacher's lesson. From this time on he never slighted anything even in a dark room.

Comment—Even the ancients were scolded if they discussed the Way of Zen and laughed involuntarily. Nowadays in the social world people hold their sides with laughter over jokes. If Zenji Tanka were to see this, what would he do?

Always crying with tears in the night

Zenji Gon of Ian was training furiously. When night came he always cried with tears and said to himself, "Today also passed so vainly. How should I train tomorrow?" He did not talk even a word among the monks.

*—The great inventor Edison said, "Genius is one percent inspiration and ninety-nine percent perspiration."

Training with effort for three years

Zenji Maido Soshin said of himself, "When I entered into the Buddha Way I had pride, thinking it easy. But after I met my teacher

Enan at Oryu Mountain I reflected on my daily life and became aware that there were many things contradicting the Law. Therefore I trained with effort for three years with steady mind, even in the coldest and the most sultry times, and finally I got freedom in each thing, no contradictions between the practice and the Law. Now for me even coughing, spitting, and swinging the arms is the meaning of why the First Patriarch came from India to China."

*—"Why did the First Patriarch, Bodhidharma, come from India to China?" is one of the Zen koans which is asking "What is the essence of Buddhism?" or "Show me the freedom, Nirvana." With assiduity we must enter into the harmonious contrasting world from the suffering contradictory world.

With a round pillow to prevent sleep

An attendant, Tetsu, used a round wooden pillow for sleeping. When he fell into sleep, the pillow rolled, and when he awoke he always had meditation. A person said, "You are doing this with too much assiduity." But the answer was, "By my nature I have little connection with Hannya. If I don't try like this I will be led by delusion."

*—If there is someone who worries over insomnia, please enjoy, you can meditate.

Not noticing the rainfall

Priest An was furious for the Way, had no time to eat or have a rest. One day he was devoting himself to the koan of A Dog while leaning against a rail. And he did not notice the rainfall until his robes were soaking wet.

*—The koan of A Dog is a basic koan to awaken for the Dharma. It came from Zenji Joshu's answer to a monk who asked him, "Is there Buddha-nature in a dog?" Because to him it seemed not, though our Sakyamuni Buddha declared that everything has Buddha-nature. But Zenji Joshu answered, "Mu" ("Not").

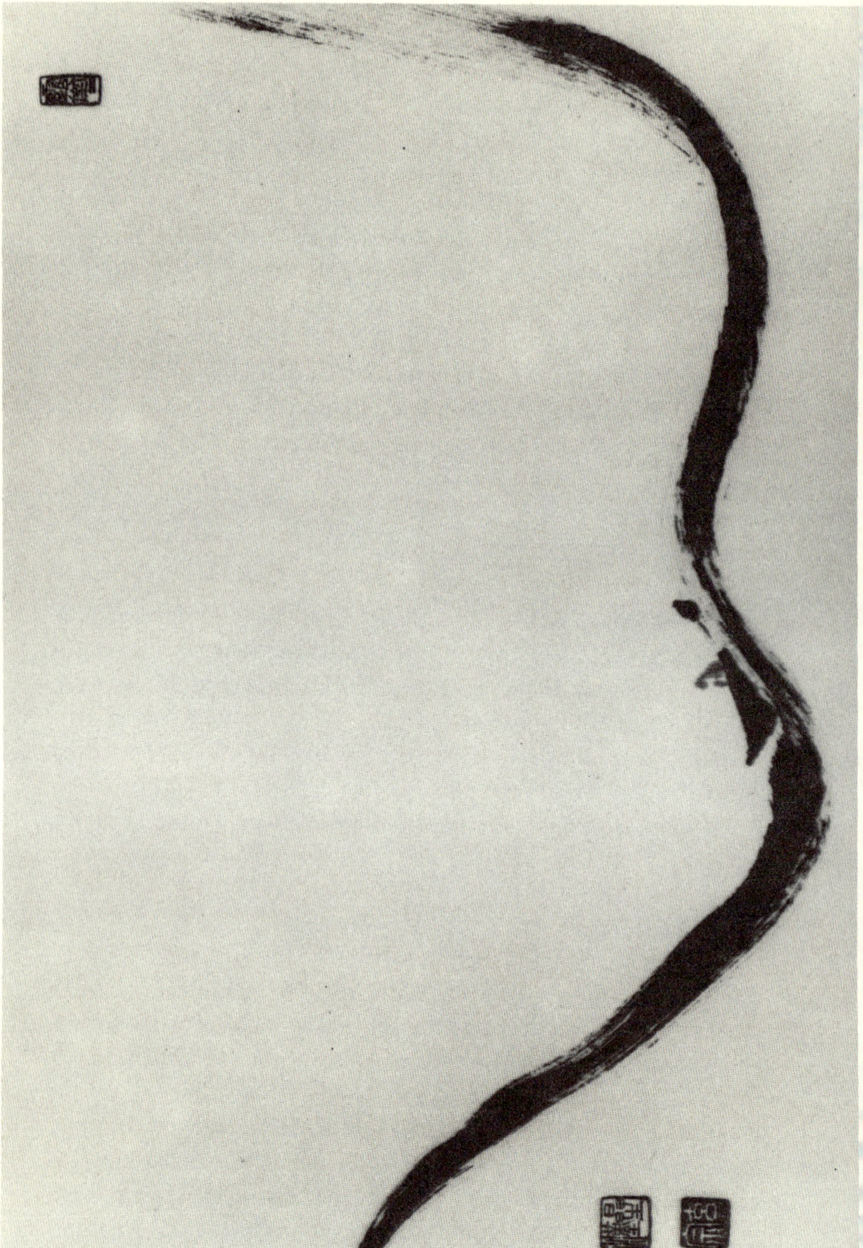

The Bodhisattva Way

Vowing not to use a bed

Zenji Shujun at Butto was training with many monks under Priest Bukkan. But his mind was foggy and he could not get any enlightenment. He despaired and said, "In all my life if I cannot get enlightenment completely, I vow I will never use a bed for sleeping." Forty-nine days passed, and he was standing leaning against a column like the person who is going into mourning for his parents. Then he could get enlightenment completely.

*—Even if you want to do so, this kind of hard training cannot be imitated while you have no Bodhisattva mind inside of you. Know that the burr of a chestnut will break open from within, not from the outside.

Throwing away letters without regret

Zenji Chihei of Tetsumen began to pilgrimage (to seek the Way). As soon as he left his native land, he was informed that his first teacher's temple burned to ash one night. When he got that letter he threw it away saying, "It makes only disturbance of one's mind, it is useless."

*—Real love and thanks to one's teacher is first to rebuild the temple in one's mind.

Vowing to train hard

Zenji Yuishin of Reigen studied at first under Soshin at Oryu with many monks and asked the Way. But he was absent-minded and could not grasp more than shadows. Then one night he vowed in front of the Buddha altar, "I must devote all my life to donating to the Law. It is to be hoped that I will open my wisdom eye and get Nirvana." From that night he read the sayings of Gensha and when he became tired he leaned over the wall, and meditated as he walked. His walking was so quick that his shoe was left behind. While he stooped to get it, suddenly he got enlightenment.

*—If there is the mind, everywhere there is enlightenment.

There was not any special occasion

Zenji Engo Kokugon trained as an attendant under Hoen at East Mountain. He studied and practiced with effort. And he himself said, "Though I stayed with many monks I had not any special occasion suddenly to get enlightenment. I could get it only by ten years sincere effort."

Comment—He said he had not any special occasion. Let me try to ask you, how many special occasions had you in a whole day, today? When can you get enlightenment?

Not forgetting even for a moment

Zenji Hochu of Bokuan studied the teachings of the Tendai Sect at the beginning. Later he wished to study the Zen Sect and met with Butsugen at Ryumon. He did not forget to study koans even for a moment. One time when he was walking by a water mill he happened to see a phrase on the cottage which read, "Always the wheel of Dharma is turning." And he got enlightenment.

Reaching the dock without noticing

Zenji Kyoko of Keiju was training under Hoko at Joshu-fusho and he practiced assiduously from morning until night. One day on business he came to a dock at Chodo after passing through Suiyo. At that time he was still in doubt about a koan and did not notice that he had reached the dock. His companion warned him, "Here is the dock!" When he became aware of it, feelings of sorrow and joy occurred alternately. He told this happening to Hoko when he came back. But Hoko said, "This thick-witted person, not yet at all." Then he obeyed his teacher's saying and devoted himself to studying the koan "Sun-facing Buddha, Moon-facing Buddha." One day when he was meditating in the hall he got enlightenment by hearing the sound of the *kaihan*.

*—The kaihan is an instrument made out of a thick rectangular wood plank which is beaten upon by a wooden hammer, used in the monastery to announce various ceremonial times. Usually on the kaihan the following stanza is written to stimulate our training:

> Death-life is the most important matter
> Mortal beings are changing rapidly
> Time does not await the person
> Be greedy for the light and shade.

The koan "Sun-facing Buddha, Moon-facing Buddha" is found in the *Records of the Sayings of Zenji Baso Doitsu* (Ma-tsu), or the third case of *The Records of Blue Rock Temple*.[6] Zenji Baso was sick. An abbot asked him, "How are you these days?" Zenji Baso replied, "Sun-facing Buddha, Moon-facing Buddha." It is said in a sutra that the life of the Sun-facing Buddha is one thousand eight hundred years; the life of the Moon-facing Buddha is only one day and one night. For solving this koan the knowledge of this saying in the sutra has no power. Zenji Baso showed the deep humanity which will not be seen even by Sakyamuni Buddha though Zenji Baso also will pass away as a mortal. By the way, your understanding of all koans must be testified to in practice and be certified by a correct teacher in sanzen.[7]

Forgetting both to eat and to sleep

At the beginning Zenji Sugaku of Shogen studied under Donge at Oan as a layman, but he could not do so clearly. Then he encouraged himself to make more effort and faced with Ketsu at Mitsu-an. He could answer for each question. Ketsu said with grief, "Your Zen is just the Zen of a box tree." Therefore he made even greater effort until he almost forgot both to eat and to sleep. Accidentally he heard that Teacher Ketsu asked a monk, "What is the meaning of 'it is not mind, it is not Buddha, it is not things'?" Overhearing this, Sugaku got enlightenment.

*—"The Zen of a box tree" is an encouragement to train hard, because a box tree will grow hardly an inch a year and, it was said, will shrink an inch a leap year. "It is not mind, it is not Buddha, it is not things" appears in the twenty-seventh koan from *Mumon-kan* as follows:

> To Priest Nansen a monk asked, "Is there the Dharma which is not preached to anyone?" Nansen replied, "Yes, there is." "Tell me, what is the Dharma which is not preached to anyone?" asked the monk. Nansen answered, "It is not mind, it is not Buddha, it is not things."

The essence of this koan is to study until you can testify to this "it" with your practical life. What is this "it"?

Forgetting to eat and dress

Zenji Koho Genmyo trained amidst many monks without lying down to sleep, and he forgot to eat and to dress, too. One time when he went to the toilet, he came out with only his undershirt on. Another time, when he opened a chest, he left without shutting it. Later when he returned to Kinzan Monastery he got great enlightenment.

Throwing off all concerns

Zenji Segu at Keppo studied from Kogon and Sekimon at the beginning. From them he got a stanza to study and had meditation devoutly all day and night, but could not make clear. Later he studied under Shigon. This teacher let him study the koan, "It is not mind, it is not Buddha, it is not things." He furiously asked the meaning of this koan, threw off all concerns and forgot both to sleep and to eat. He was like a dead person. One evening he was meditating and night came. Then he heard the next monk chanting *Shodo-ka*, ("The Song of Proving the Way"). When the phrases "Do not take the delusion off and do not seek the truth" were chanted he got enlightenment, which was like unloading a heavy burden. And he made a pair of phrases,

> In the night I forgot in a flash
> the finger pointing at the moon,
> And empty sky thrust out the round sun
> which is red.

Shutting the gate and studying hard

A prime minister, Sozai, was studying from Zenji Bansho and he drove away the miscellaneous affairs of his home and refused to see visitors. Not a day passed, even the coldest or hottest, in which he did not study. He burned oil for light in order to continue his training into the night and stopped sleeping, forgot to eat. After three years passed finally he was certified.

Comment—He took care like this and he was certified about the Way like this. He is worthy of being called in the social world a Bodhisattva. Eating meat and on a full stomach visiting the Zen priest to talk about Zen—what is the value of that?

*—Without Cause there is no Effect. If there is no Effect, we should make the Cause while we are human beings.

Bumping the head against a post

Zenji Hon of Chuho was studying hard every day and night under Shikan at Koho as an attendant. When he got tired, he bumped his head against a post. One day while chanting the Diamond Sutra he came to the phrase "helps Tathagata" and he became enlightened dimly. But he said to himself, "My enlightenment is not yet reaching the extreme." And he trained further without laziness to clear away the doubt. When he saw a running stream, he got great enlightenment.

Comment—He said to himself, "My enlightenment is not yet

reaching the extreme." That's why he could reach the ultimate extremity by more training. So many modern trainers are satisfied to return to their homes even though they are only on the way of training. What a sorrowful matter it is!

Doing hard training behind a shut gate

Zenji Honzen of Dokuho shut himself up at Iku'kei. For sleeping he had no bed and only one chair, and aimed to get enlightenment. One night he fell into a sleep so deep that he could not awake until midnight. Then he took the chair away and continued by standing. But this time he fell into sleep leaning on the wall. Then he vowed not to lean on the wall and was walking in the air as if swimming. His physical strength was exhausted and sleepiness became stronger and stronger. Finally he cried in front of the altar and reproved himself severely by every means. And he could progress in his study each day. When he heard the sound of a bell, suddenly he got freedom. He made a stanza:

It is absolutely quiet and any human power falls short of it.
It has no beginning to be studied, and it roars, is like thunder.
The one sound which shakes the earth has not a clue.
It was the first time to be awakened from my dream
    when a skull was broken.

Without lying down

Zenji Hokon of Hekiho studied under Kaishin at Fukai. The teacher gave him the koan "All Dharmas return to one." He doubted on this koan for three years. When by chance he was picking vegetables he stopped moving for a while. Teacher Kaishin asked to him, "Did you enter into samadhi?" "I have relationship with neither samadhi nor perturbation, he replied." Then Teacher Kaishin asked, "Who is he who has relationship with neither samadhi nor perturbation?" Hokon showed a vessel made of bamboo. But the teacher did not yet certify him. And Hokon studied harder and did not lie down, continued to meditate while seven days passed. One day by hearing the sound of woodcutting he got enlightenment.

*—The most enjoyable and at the same time the most suffering time is when a teacher says, "not yet," "still more." The koan "All Dharmas return to one" can be found in *Joshu Shinzai Zenji Goroku (The Sayings of Zenji Joshu Shinzai)*, or *Hekigan-roku*, the forty-fifth case:

> A monk asked Joshu, "All Dharmas return to one. Where does the one return to?" Joshu replied, "When I was at Sei Prefecture I made a coat which weighed only seven ounces."

Dharma has three literal meanings. One is the Universal Law as truth; second is the Law as taught by Buddha; third is phenomena as existence.

Continuing alone to train blindly

Zenji Musai Myogo of Seishoku when he trained at the beginning could not read even a four-fingers sized book. Only blindly, intently he continued, and finally got enlightenment.

Comment—Such a way to train is very good. But while you don't study the teachings of Buddha, you should not imitate this.

All of the above I translated hoping you will encourage your sincere training. I did not explain in so much detail because my purpose was only to show how Patriarchs in old times loved the training. Though I use the word "study" so often, it does not mean to read books or think dualistically, but rather to enter Dhyana-paramita.

The fifth paramita, Dhyana, is translated into English as "meditation," in Japanese, *Zen*. Briefly described, Dhyana is the practical living so as to present the freedom everywhere every moment by awakening the self, which is the universe, the Law, through the acts of concentration on the object until all contradictory, dualistic, mutual opposition disappears, and alternately through the acts of coming back from such absolute world to the relative world. Originally Dhyana meant "to think quietly." This meaning comes from the Buddhism of ancient India in the age of the Upanishads before the appearance of Sakyamuni Buddha. The people of that time questioned the purpose of our human life amidst many sufferings, such as hot weather, short life, hunger, fighting, and so on. And they asked, what is the universe?

Even now we should think about how we should live. After spending most of our life, even if we notice that our way to live was a great mistake, it is too late. And if we don't notice, that is only worse. That's why we should think about our life or the universe quietly and sincerely. If the people of ancient India thought in this way, should not we too, as cultivated, modern human beings, think so?

They chose a suitable place, such as under the trees or by the streamside in the forest, and knew by their experience that zazen is the most comfortable position, one most easily continued for a long time, and in this way easy for getting quietness for their meditation. And finally they reached the thought that Dhyana is the purpose of our life. Because, they thought, the noumenon of the great universe, *Brahman,* and the essence of the individual, *Atman,* are one body. (This has been called an idealistic monism in modern philosophy.) Further they thought from this original principle all things will occur, and human life, which should be absorbed into Dhyana, will transmigrate according to karma. Therefore the highest purpose of human life, achieved through stoic Dhyana practice, is to be delivered after death from endless transmigration (*Rinne* in Japanese) in order to live in the immortal, unchangeable world, *Brahma-loka,* by awakening to the truth that Brahman and Atman are one body.

Our Sakyamuni Buddha practiced this Dhyana and through his hard training he built his standpoint. Though he did not utterly deny the Atman, he thought that it has no ultimate, immortal, unchangeable, settled essence, but rather that all beings are occurring by mutual relation and Cause and Effect. Consequently for Sakyamuni Buddha there were not any dualistic oppositions such as body and mind, material and soul, or Brahman and Atman. And Dhyana practice was not the purpose for him but the necessary method to complete human life, humanity. Therefore by practicing Dhyana he could avoid the vice of falling into the inactive, dead quietness, or the darkness of our reason and body, and for him there was no need to hope to be born in heaven after death because there was heaven on this earth.

Generally, however, Indian Dhyana was only one of three important Buddhist practices, the other two being Sila and Prajna. This means Dhyana itself was not given so much meaning as a religious act without the practice of Sila and Prajna. However, when Buddhism entered into China, this Dhyana was called *Ch'in* and given deeper meaning by the understanding that Dhyana and Prajna are not separate things. While there is Dhyana there is Prajna, and while there is Prajna there is Dhyana. This understanding of Dhyana was very much advanced by many patriarchs of the Ch'in Sect. They could say Dhyana is the essence, the mind of Buddha, of Buddhism. Naturally Dhyana had practical power as the expression of Prajna and Sila. Therefore in China daily life was considered important as Buddhist life itself. Dhyana which meant 'to think quietly', became Ch'in: 'to live practically'. Therefore the Sixth Patriarch Eno said, "Everywhere, practice the one mind through the acts of walking, standing, sitting, and lying down." This is Ch'in. He said as well about zazen, "Sitting means there is not any interference and the mind will not be perturbed. Meditation means to see the original nature and not be confused by anything." And, "Separating from the forms on the outside will be called Ch'in and not being confused within will be called samadhi."

And Zenji Hyakujo Ekai[8] said, "One day without work should be one day without eating," which means work is the natural act of Prajna itself, and working is Dhyana. Zenji Nansen said, "Normal, daily mind is the Way." So it was that when Dhyana entered into

China, it had the meaning 'to practice as Prajna nature,' which is Ch'in.

In Japan, Dhyana, Ch'in, was called Zen and had a great influence of Japanese culture. This means, I think, that Dhyana in Japan meant not only to practice as Prajna, but meant 'to live beautifully' as well. Therefore Zen made Japanese culture great in such forms as gardening, tea-ceremony, Noh play, Haiku-poem, Zen-sumi painting, and even swordsmanship, archery, karate, judo and so on.[9]

Thus though we use the word Dhyana, (Ch'in, Zen), it is difficult to explain it because Dhyana is also the living acts of human beings which depend on their understanding. I think from now on we should give to Dhyana the meaning of 'to live freely'. I am hoping such a kind of Dhyana, Zen, will be built up in America. We should be able to live freely in any time or place. We must be free even from beautiful culture or art if it binds us. We should free ourselves even from good philosophy if it binds us. Of course if it is an ugly, bad thing, we should be free from it. Fortunately we are originally free; we are being because we are free. Within the Hannya Sutra this will be further explained.

We have no need to seek freedom, we must only awaken to our free being. How can we awaken to it must be our most interesting question. The answer comes by practicing the Six Paramitas as a Bodhisattva. But even though we try to practice those six at one time, it is very difficult to do so. One of the six must be chosen and practiced with concentration. If you do this, all the others will be practiced naturally, but gradually. Humanity means to practice one of the Six Paramitas ceaselessly. Among these Six Paramita practices, Dhyana is the easiest to practice and to live as a Bodhisattva, because you can have meditation anytime, anywhere, even if you are in the sickbed. And you do not need any money, instruments, special knowledge or preparation. Then here I will introduce to you the most common way to practice Dhyana. You can use this introduction for your life according to your own situation.

Always, if there is a person who wants to practice Dhyana, he is already training as a Bodhisattva. The Bodhisattva should have great love for all sentient beings. He vows to help all sentient beings and never try to live in Nirvana by himself only. For other people we will have Dhyana, which is really doing for ourselves as well. Then if you determine to do so, zazen is the most basic way to practice Dhyana. Because for Dhyana practice, quietness of the body and mind is very important. Without quietness, we cannot awaken for our original nature which is the universe itself. It is just like trying to get a jewel on the bottom of a stream. If you don't calm the water, you cannot see it. But this jewel has its own life. If you are in the quietness, it will work as its nature. And you will know the work of this jewel is your self, or the life of the universe itself. Letting it work as it likes is the freedom of your self. Getting quietness of body and mind means letting this jewel, our original nature, create its life as it likes.

Even in social matters, if you don't have such quietness during which you can at least hear your heart beating, you will not be able to do any good work. If you are a musician, while playing your instrument you should hear your breathing. If you are not quiet because of anger or worry how can you play beautifully? To create any great thing, you should have this quietness. For that purpose, running is worse than walking, and sitting is better than walking. And even for sitting, sitting on a chair in a posture like Rodin's statue The Thinker is very different from sitting on the floor. The former is a very good posture for thinking dualistically with logic or speculation or analysis. But now we want to know before logic, before analysis, we want to know our original nature itself. This means forgetting our thinking and being in the origin. For that if we sit on the floor it is much better, if we can sit in the field it is still better. If you experiment with each of these positions, you will see that to get the quietness, sitting in the field, directly touching your body to nature is the best way.

I have heard that a storyteller said, "Making a standing audience cry is almost impossible. Making an audience sitting on chairs cry is difficult. But making an audience sitting on the floor cry is easy." The third kind of audience is purer for its original nature and not egoistically or dualistically thinking. If you understand this fact, try sitting on the floor. And if you cannot do so for some reason, while you hope to some day, you can have another posture as close as possible.

About eating food, simply know that a stomach eighty percent full is best. I am not sure why, but in my observation of myself, eating only vegetables and fruits makes the practice of Dhyana much easier than on days of eating meat or fish. Please avoid meditating in the time just after and before your meal. As for sleeping, also don't have too much or too little sleep. Needless to say, Dhyana practice is not to sleep but to awake beyond our sleepy thinking. Therefore our body and mind must be in very good, fresh condition. You should choose a quiet, clean place but not under direct sun or wind. If you burn a thin, favorite incense your mind and body and place will be harmonized very well. For your dress you will wear loose clothes, loosen your belt, and take off your necktie, watch, rings, and so on. If you wear glasses or contact lenses put them aside.

While I am talking about these comfortable conditions, you may wonder what happened about the stoic assiduity of such people as were described in *Zen-kan-saku-shin*. But know that no one forced any of them to do as they did; they acted from their own desire. It was impossible for them to stop doing so, because of their spontaneous wish with the enjoyment of Bodhisattvahood. Therefore while you have not such desire, even if you do such formal training, you will not get anything except what stoicism is. They did not do any stoical training for themselves. If a mother must awaken every three or four hours to nurse her baby and does so out of stoicism, what a strange creature she is! Even though they got bodily tiredness to the extreme, they had great formless enjoyment. Until you have such enjoyment in yourself, practicing by following your honest desire is much more fruitful training.

Next is about the body. Our body is one of the most important resources for training the Bodhisattva Way. It is said, "Without body there is no Dharma body." We should train with our body and our body will be made by our training. All forms are for training and training makes all forms. Then at first harmonizing our body is necessary. This is done by cross-legged sitting. If you cross both of your legs it is called full lotus flower posture, and if you use only one leg put on the other thigh it is half lotus flower posture. In either case you should sit so that both kneecaps and coccyx touch the floor directly. Your neck and backbone must stand so that if you had put a coin on top of your head and it were dropped straight down it would come out from your anus. Then your body will sit solidly like a tetrahedron. Swing your body a few times forward and backward and to the right and left like a pendulum, and as you let it stop naturally it will stand correctly. Of course you can use a thick cushion to sit on, but please notice that it should not be so soft that your hips sink in or so colorful as to disturb your eyes. By the way, there is a saying, "While you cannot sit with full lotus flower posture, you cannot say you are doing zazen. You cannot talk about Zen before you enter into samadhi." This will become good encouragement for your training and for keeping your honesty. You should be eager to try to sit with full lotus flower posture, but in my opinion it is enough to sit in half lotus flower posture. The important thing is not cross-legged sitting itself but to harmonize your body comfortably and enter into samadhi. Therefore it has been said that "Zazen is the easy gate to enter the Dharma."

As for your hands, hold the right hand with the left hand lightly and both thumbs will face each other inside. Rest both arms around the abdomen. You may put a little power on both your thumbs, but don't apply any strength anywhere. For that purpose, after you are sitting and holding your hands, you can lift your shoulders up and lower them a few times to relax them. Since old times it was said that the right hand receives the left hand, both palms face up, the tips of both thumbs touch each other, and so on. But for new trainers such an empty ring formed by both hands is not helpful. It seems rather a silly complication. For concentration of your mind and body, if you hold your hands as I have suggested it is good enough.

Well, if you get this posture, next take off your power from head, neck, shoulders, and stomach in that order while keeping your correct posture. From your navel up don't apply any power and naturally your center of gravity will be settled in your abdomen. After you have come this far, reflect on your posture one more time. If both of your ears are not positioned straight above your shoulders, your body is bending to the right or left.

As much as possible have meditation with friends, with family. We will enter into the deep world by Dhyana practice but we should not forget that the social mutual relation is also an important thing. About this point, I will enjoy if you meditate with other people, though if you do not have anyone at least you are with Buddha. Still, you should think you are sitting in the wide field or on the top of a great mountain, even though you have only a small space. Quietly, grandly, and alertly sit down.

About a hundred years ago there was a swordsman named Yamaoka. His house, it seems, was poor and there were many mice in the ceiling, kitchen, and floors. But as soon as he began his meditation, all the mice became quiet and remained silent while he was meditating. His wife felt it was very strange and commented about it to her husband. Yamaoka did not feel any pride but rather felt a kind of embarassment, and he said, "How sorrowful! My meditation has value only as mouse poison," and he tried to attain a more calm meditation. Later, upon his shoulders, knees, or around him many mice played cheerfully.

This episode tells us that we should train furiously until we get the real quietness.

Your mouth will shut naturally and both top and bottom teeth touch each other slightly. The tip of the tongue should touch the upper gum. Your eyes will see about three feet in front of you. Then without moving your head, lower your gaze. Don't try to see something and also don't try not to see anything. In this way your eyes are half-opening Buddha eyes.

Here I would like to introduce a related story from the *Den-to-roku (Record of the Transmission of the Lamp)*, for persons who cannot have correct sitting posture because of illness or some misfortune.

Zenji Nangaku Ejo[10] asked to Baso Doitsu, "What on earth are you doing so much zazen for?"

"I am hoping to become Buddha," came the reply.

Instantly Zenji Nangaku picked up a piece of tile and began to polish it with a rock in the garden.

Doitsu asked, "My Zenji, what are you doing to do?"

"I am hoping to make a mirror by polishing this."

"How can you make a mirror by polishing a piece of tile?"

"You can not become Buddha by doing meditation, can you?", Zenji asked.

"Then what should I do?" Doitsu asked.

"When you try to advance the cow cart and it does not move, which is better, to whip the cow or whip the cart?"

". . ." Doitsu could not say anything, and Zenji continued,

"If you are studying zazen, it means you are studying the sitting Buddha. But Zen is not in sitting or lying down. And Buddha has no certain form such as sitting. Therefore you should study the Law which is not bound by convention to anything. If you say you are studying the sitting Buddha by doing zazen it means you are killing the Buddha. If you are bound by convention to the form of sitting, you can't attain the truth."

If you can make the quiet, harmonized body, you will then breathe deeply a few times. At first, open your mouth wide and without using throat or chest but with only the contracting power of your abdomen, breathe out slowly and long until your chest becomes empty. The air and the inside of your abdomen will directly touch. Just after you breathe out, loosen the contraction of your abdomen while shutting your mouth. Naturally by the outside pressure air will enter into your body. Drink air through your chest until the air fills your abdomen. When you have drawn in enough air, keep it a moment and by straightening your waist the air will settle very well in your abdomen. At this time you should neither bear down nor use strenth, but should shut your anus. And just before you suffer from holding your breath, breathe out again.

Please notice that this breathing is a really great matter for us, our direct communication with the universe. If you stop either breath, out or in, you will die. I think we human beings must think more carefully about our breathing.

In this way if you make good preparation of your body, next is the harmonizing of your mind. For that, counting breaths and studying koans are the most excellent ways. But about the koan method I will not talk because if you don't visit a good teacher and study from him every day, it usually does not succeed. If you want koan study, please visit a correct teacher.

Counting breath means that while keeping your zazen posture you will count your breath slowly from one to ten and again from one to ten, continuously. If you breathe in and out one time, it will be counted as one. The important point is that the connection of the breaths out and in should be done very smoothly, like drawing an imaginary figure 8. And don't separate your breath and the number being counted, or the one who is counting and the breathing. How much you can unify these three is the subject of your zazen training. Counting your breath in this way can be continuous through all of your life.

There is another way to count your breath, which is to count only 'one' for your breathing in and 'two' for your breathing out, repeatedly. This way has the same effect as the previous way. The only important thing is that the subject which is you, and the object which is the number, and the breath must be melted so that there is no distinction between them. Entering into samadhi is the essence of zazen training. Finally, when you finish zazen, you should not stand suddenly. Release your mind and open your mouth calmly and swing your body forward and backward, to the left and right, and slowly stand. This is in order to continue your Dhyana in your active life.

In all of the above concerning the way to practice Dhyana. I did not talk about so many virtues of zazen or small questionable matters, because zazen is only for living as a Bodhisattva.

The sixth paramita is Prajna. I have given some previous

explanation of Prajna, and I shall be mentioning it again. I have talked about the Six Paramitas. Bodhisattva means the person who practices the Six Paramitas. Avalokitesvara is also one Bodhisattva. Avalokitesvara (Kannon) is the crystallization of the mercy with sorrow *(jihi)* which is the necessary hope of human beings, and the wisdom *(chie)* of Hannya which is the highest spirituality of human beings. Each person has this Avalokitesvara in his inner mind. And Avalo— kitesvara helps the people who want to live the correct way which is the Bodhisattva Way in this contradictory world filled with suffering.

Though 'God explained is not God any more,' if I dare explain Avalokitesvara literally, *Avaloka (Avalokita)* means "to look" and *iśvara* means "freedom," or *śvara* means "sound." Therefore, Avalokitesvara means "the one who looks at freedom, and at once the one who freely helps all sentient beings by looking at the sound of suffering sentient beings."[11]

The meaning of "the one who looks at freedom" is that one should be as freedom itself, not see freedom objectively. While there is the subject who sees and the objects which are seen, it is not yet real looking. Because still there is a medium between the subject and the object. Naturally, perfect looking will not be done with our physical eyes, but with spiritual eye. "Freedom" is being "as freedom itself," which means it does not depend on any surrounding circumstances. Being as suchness itself is freedom. In fact, real freedom can not be attained by getting something from outside of yourself, or by taking away something from outside of yourself. We can get real freedom only by recognizing our being which is freedom itself. Our being is the acts of freedom. But as soon as the acts of freedom become the result of the acts of freedom, we are not free anymore. Therefore, letting the acts of freedom of our being continue is the hopeful way to live. Letting your nature be as suchness and taking away all the dust which is the result of the acts of freedom is the best way to live in the freedom. In other words, all forms exist because they are the acts of freedom itself. But when we have forms, whatever they are, they restrain our freedom. Therefore, destroying all forms, not being attached to them, but letting the acts of freedom itself continue, is the best way to live. Speaking simply, eternally continue to live the creative life which is like a running stream, never stopping, or like a turning water mill, never freezing with ice. For affirming your free life, you should deny your self, which is the result of the acts of freedom. In this light it must be common sense that the death of Christ on the Cross is the Resurrection itself. These are not miracles at all. Not only Christ, but all sincere people must die on the Cross and be reborn every day, each hour.[12]

". . . freely helps all sentient beings by looking at the sound of suffering sentient beings." This means to awaken human beings to their freedom. In our mind there are many sentient beings already, such as anger, envy, love, hate, and all delusions. If we see the real freedom, already we are helped. Not only ourselves; we would like to help all other sentient beings. The more we help ourselves the more we help others. If a person does not help others, he is not helping himself, sorrowfully. But Avalokitesvara could help himself perfectly, therefore he can help others also. Therefore it was said in the Lotus Flower Sutra that "Bodhisattva Mujinni asked to the Buddha. 'Why, for what reasons, was Kan-ze-on (Avalokitesvara) named so?' Buddha replied, 'Good man, if there are innumerable, one hundred times one thousand times one million times one billion sentient beings who are suffering in various ways, by hearing this Kan-ze-on if they chant the name of Kan-ze-on with heart and soul, they will be freed from sufferings instantly by the looking of Kan-ze-on.'"

When you understand this sutra in the subjective way, you yourself have the Avalokitesvara, and by the concentration, Dhyana, of looking at Avalokitesvara, you will be free from all sufferings. When you understand this sutra in the objective way, you ask the helping of Avalokitesvara and he will help all your sufferings. In fact we cannot distinguish between the subjective and objective ways. Truth is at one time both, and working as Avalokitesvara. Then we can say believing God means believing our original mind. Believing our original mind means believing God. Faith is the effort to awaken for our origin. After all God is wherever we realize.

The Bodhisattva Way 77

With this understanding if you see the next words of the Lotus Flower Sutra you can really have thanks to Avalokitesvara, to the world, to our beings. Avalokitesvara is saying, "While I practice the Bodhisattva Way, I will help all of the sufferings of sentient beings if they chant my name while they are desperate in various sufferings, helpless in solitary grief, because I will hear with the ears of Heaven, will see with the eyes of heaven, whenever, wherever they are. I will not become Buddha eternally while there is even a person who does not get rid of his sufferings." So he declared, clearly.

And Avalokitesvara has ten great vows which are found in the "Great Mercy With Sorrow Dharani Sutra" *(Daihi-shu)*:

1. It is hoped that I will know quickly all of the Dharmas.
2. That I will get soon the eye of Prajna.
3. That I will help quickly all sentient beings.
4. That I will get soon the good expedients.
5. That I will ride quickly the boat of Nirvana.
6. That I will cross over soon the ocean of suffering.
7. That I will get quickly the way of Sila and Dhyana.
8. That I will climb soon the mountain of Nirvana.
9. That I will understand quickly the house of nothing to do.
10. That I will be soon as the Dharma body itself.

If we chant this Great Mercy With Sorrow Dharani Sutra, we can escape from the fifteen kinds of unwelcome evil death and can live in the fifteen kinds of hopeful good life. Without real practice, you cannot say this is nonsense. In fact, if you live as a Bodhisattva there are no sufferings, there is only enjoyment, except for sorrow with mercy for other ignorant sentient beings.

The Fifteen Kinds of Evil Death are:

1. Death by the sufferings of starvation.
2. Death by punishment.
3. Death by revenge.
4. Death by fighting in war.
5. Death by the attack of beasts, such as tigers or wolves.

6. Death by the toxin of beasts, such as vipers or scorpions.
7. Death by water and fire.
8. Death by poison.
9. Death by poisoning.
10. Death by madness or loss of one's mind.
11. Death by falling trees or landslide.
12. Death by the attack of bad men.
13. Death by an evil spirit or demon.
14. Death by the cursed disease.
15. Death by suicide.

If you know and practice the Bodhisattva Way you have no need to worry about death from such causes. If you cannot practice the Bodhisattva Way at least believe Avalokitesvara's love with sorrow, and live brightly. Of course you will not die by air crash or car accident but will die naturally in bed or doing your professional work. Or you can die after writing a poem while sitting, as Zennists are accustomed to do.

The Fifteen Kinds of Good Life are:

1. Wherever you are, you can meet with a good master.
2. Always you can be in a good country.
3. Always you can have good opportunity.
4. You can face with good friends always.
5. All of your body is healthy all the time.
6. You can train the Bodhisattva Way very well.
7. You will not act against the precepts.
8. All your family and relatives keep the friendship.
9. Always you have enough property.
10. You can get help and respect from other people always.
11. Your property will not be plundered.
12. You can accomplish whatever you hope to do.
13. Gods protect and help you always.
14. Where you are born you can see Buddha and hear the Dharma.
15. Whatever you hear, you can enlighten to the Dharma.

The Bodhisattva Way 79

Well, there are many sufferings and satisfactions, if we try to count them. But simply if you practice the Bodhisattva Way, you can get rid of all suffering and you can be in the happiness. Because you are practicing Prajna, Hannya.

Then now see the quotation from the Hannya Sutra, "When the Bodhisattva Avalokitesvara practiced the deep Prajna-paramita." For us this one word "practice" is the most important word in all of this sutra. Without this one word, practice, the whole sutra, the whole philosophy, the whole world, becomes a bubble of air, and you will become a ghost which has only shadow and no real existence and depends on others but not on himself.

As the great philosopher Immanuel Kant was always saying to his students, "Do not study philosophy, but study to do philosophy. I will teach you to do philosophy, but not philosophy." Someone has said, "Rather become the thin Socrates than a fat pig." But without feet, even if you become the thin Socrates, it is no better than being a fat pig. I am hoping for my body to be like that of a lion for practicing the Way and my mind to be like Avalokitesvara for his Hannya and mercy with sorrow. Even though I say "practice," it is not a special conduct. From morning to night, from night to morning, if you try to know your own mind, already that is the practice of the Six Paramitas. Knowing yourself is the key to it all. Study, study yourself, study your original nature, original face.

IV Why We Suffer

he perceived that the five Skandhas are all empty and was freed from all sufferings.

sho ken go un kai ku, do its sai ku yaku.

While we are living, there are sufferings. It is not so easy to enjoy while saying that having suffering is the proof that we are living. To a person who is in the midst of suffering, even though it seems a trivial suffering to others, it is the most important thing to be solved. For a baby, even the moment's absence of mother is a large suffering. He will cry as if the world has ended.

In an old Chinese story, there was a person who worried about what he should do if the earth broke open. And he could not work, could not be satisfied in his everyday life. He became ill. He had a friend who worried so much about what he should do for his friend that he himself could not feel satisfaction, could not sleep even a night. Maybe people will laugh over this story, but in fact most people are suffering with this kind of imaginary or deluded thought. And the older we get, the more we have responsibility with its increase of suffering. We can not live only for our self, like a baby. No baby will commit suicide. Always good, sincere people increase these sufferings according to their realization of responsibility or love to others. At least the president of a country must have the sufferings of all citizens as his suffering.

Our Avalokitesvara has the greatest sufferings which are the sufferings of all sentient beings in the universe. He will take all sufferings as his, without exception, unconditionally, without contract. But he is freed from all sufferings by perceiving that the Five *Skandhas* are all empty and he is teaching us to be freed in the same way. The Five Skandhas means everything inside or outside of the universe, all Dharmas. All of the phenomenal world can be classified within these Five Skandhas, which means all beings are grasped in five ways. Literally skandha means "gathering" or "the harmony of many things." Originally Buddhism explained this world as being made by the harmony of many things which can be divided into two classes, the form and the formless form. One is material and the other is mind. The mind can be divided to four which are sensation, thought, volition, and consciousness. These physical and mental gatherings are the Five Skandhas. Certainly we can analyze in more detail, but this was not Sakyamuni Buddha's interest. If people can understand that all Five Skandhas are empty, his purpose will be accomplished.

When all things are observed as materialistic or sensual matter, that is *rūpa-skandha* ("form"). For instance, our bodies are form. Each of our bodies was made by the harmony of many things which have been observed since old times as being composed with the characters of the "great four elements": the greatness of earth which has the hard character like bone, the greatness of water which has the wet character like blood, the greatness of fire which has the heated character able to keep temperature, and the greatness of wind which has the moving character to make the body grow by the movement of blood and food from here to there.

Vedana-skandha ("sensation") is the way to recognize things sensibly. In the form there are five organs *(pañcendriyāni)* which are eyes, ears, nose, tongue, and body. The objects of these five organs are matter (or color), sound, smell, taste, and feelings such as cold or warmth or hardness or softness. All things which are received by the five organs are named sensation, and this sensation can be roughly divided to three: enjoyment, suffering, and between the two.

Saṃjñā-skandha ("thought") is a kind of mental activity which is exemplified by its character of taking images. When the five objects are received by the five organs, thought will arise. For instance, by seeing the sun rise through a green forest, our mind becomes bright and feels the fresh enjoyment of life. But by seeing the sun set over a hill with a ruined house, our mind becomes dark and feels the sorrow of life. Or by seeing the faces or dress of people we feel beauty or ugliness. All of these are called thought.

Saṃskāra-skandha ("volition") is used to describe all mental actions, such as willing or deciding or choosing. Visiting Washington to see the cherry blossoms or going to a shop to buy furniture are actions. These actions which are moving in each moment are not done only by our human mind and body, for in fact all beings of the world are acting, moving. Such actions are volition.

The fifth Skandha, *vijñāna-skandha* ("consciousness"), is the general name for the mind which will discriminate or judge various things. It was made by gathering all of the above four Skandhas and can include any kind of profound works of mind. Except for this consciousness, human beings and animals or plants or insentient beings such as rocks or helium are not so different. But this consciousness makes a big difference and makes us worthy of being called by ourselves "Man, the lord of creation," even persons fully covered with delusion.

We have this consciousness. Therefore we have worship for Buddha or God and respect each other and want to train in the Bodhisattva Way.

Anyway, as I have described above, only form is a material Dharma and the other four are mental Dharmas. Although volition extends to both, it belongs to the mental Dharma. And of the mental Dharmas, consciousness is the essence of the mind and controls all others. Therefore we call it the king of the mind under which the other three mental Dharmas have the relation of servitude as possessions of the king of the mind. If I show all of these relations in a diagram, it will be arranged like this:

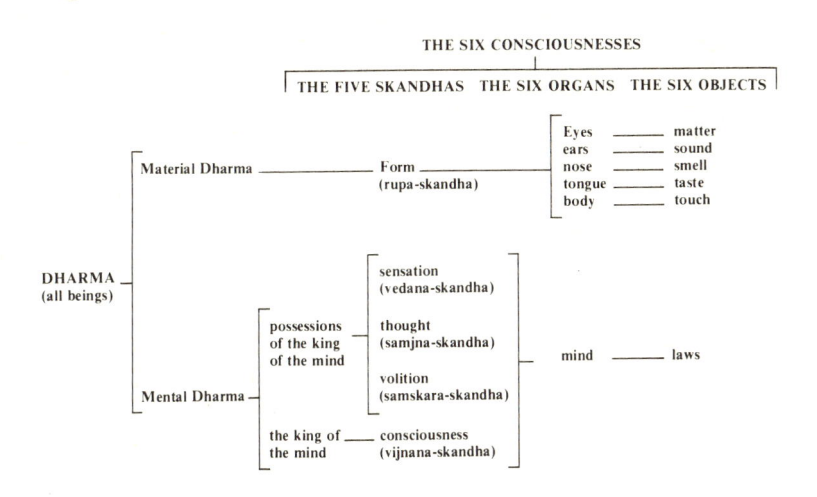

```
                              THE SIX CONSCIOUSNESSES
                   ┌──────────────────────────────────────────────┐
                   │ THE FIVE SKANDHAS   THE SIX ORGANS   THE SIX OBJECTS │
                                                 ┌ Eyes  ──────── matter
                                                 │ ears  ──────── sound
         Material Dharma ──────────── Form ──────┤ nose  ──────── smell
                                   (rupa-skandha)│ tongue ─────── taste
                                                 └ body  ──────── touch

                                        ┌ sensation
                                        │ (vedana-skandha)
                         ┌ possessions  │ thought
                         │ of the king  ┤ (samjna-skandha)
                         │ of the mind  │ volition            mind ──────── laws
         Mental Dharma ──┤              │ (samskara-skandha)
                         │
                         │ the king of ─── consciousness
                         └ the mind       (vijnana-skandha)
```

DHARMA (all beings)

Our bodies were made with these Five Skandhas and all of the universe is also made with these Five Skandhas. Therefore if we understand that our bodies are empty, we can also see that all of the universe is empty. Naturally we can be freed from any kind of suffering. Where are there sufferings?

All modern people at least know as knowledge that everything is changing, and, by the help of science, that there is no ultimate existence. But unfortunately they cannot see this truth with their physical eyes, cannot hear it with their physical ears. And while knowing this truth in their brain, in practice they are thinking that they are existing.

Generally, thinking that our bodies are existing eternally as such is the beginning of our illusion. Our bodies are the momentary harmony of the Five Skandhas by the Effect of the Cause of our parents. And this harmony is changing every moment. Therefore there is not any ultimate existence but only moving, changing acts of beings. Still if someone wants to keep his body as itself, he is trying to strain the Universal Law. Which means he is trying to deny his own being, because his being is depending on the Universal Law. And even though he is getting sufferings, we should say he is crying while seeking water in the water, trying to get his head while having his head. How comical and sorrowful a misery it is! Not only trying to keep his body, money, women, prosperity, and so on, but also angering, hating others.

All the world is one, which is empty. There is not two, except in our delusion. In one empty garden people are fighting with their delusions, such as South or North, black or white, East or West, good or bad, and so on. While people don't recognize this emptiness in this world, peace will not visit. Even when someone shouts, "Peace—No more war!" he himself is already making the delusive contrast. As long as there is contrast, war will not end; war is a natural phenomenon in the contrastable world. Rev. Kuya (d. 972) made a poem:

> In this world there is not a thing
> Which is mine,
> Even this, my body, I should
> Return to the soil.

When I was a child I somehow was a coward and afraid of everything. At my house the toilet was outside as an independent building. Whenever Nature called me, I asked my mother or father to come with me. Especially after evening was terrible. All buildings were, it seemed for me, dark monsters, and shaking bamboo forest seemed trying to hold me. The moonlight through branches was shining devils' eyes. In such a time, if a mouse ran past across my feet, I almost fainted. So often I could not begin my work while standing in front of the pee basin, worrying about what was behind me or around the well or on the other side of the gate. Because I thought unwelcome things will not always come in front of my eyes. If my sharpened ears heard an owl crying, already I was running into the house on the way of my work.

But when I entered into elementary school, my parents declared to me that they would not come to the toilet with me anymore. Of course I entreated their help and explained my fear of the monsters until they themselves almost began to become afraid, but they decided not to help me and began to anger and insult me. Finally I thought that making the enemy inside the house would make more trouble for me.

Then I had to protect myself. And I polished a small knife, and made an imaginary pistol from a branch to conceal in my pocket. For a few days, my self-encouragement was a bright idea. But soon I noticed that my monsters began to have machine guns. For that I hoped a strong thief or murderer would enter into the garden of my house, and I decided by myself smartly that he would fight with my monsters. Because in those days I had heard that many thieves had entered into my village and that police were searching everywhere. With this influence of an imaginary good thief or murderer to help me, even now I feel a kind of friendship for those people.

But unfortunately the news that those thieves were caught by police came to my house. With the shock of disappointment about their lack of strength I could not go to school for three days. My parents worried and brought me to a doctor whose customers were only robust peasants. Naturally he failed to examine me correctly and gave many suggestions of the possible illness, such as catarrh of the stomach or intestines.

In fact my family was poor, with no food, and in the daytime, which was for me a completely different peaceful time from the night, I was searching for my food in the graveyard. Though it may have been that I had such an illness, the real cause was not food but unnameable monsters. This doctor solemnly, but with rather inner enjoyment, judged and said to my parents who were showing full trust in him in their worrying about me, "If this boy does not enter a hospital within a week, he will not have the seven years old birthday." I was between my parents and thought, "I am already seven years old. Should I ask him why will I die last year?" But from the next room his assistant and nurse and secretary and wife scolded him, "My dear, he is already seven years old!" The doctor did not move even an eyebrow and said with the same solemnness, but with rather inner enjoyment,

"If this boy is not sent to a hospital within a week, he will not have his twelfth birthday."

From that day I had the same dream every night in which I was inside a coffin being carried to the graveyard by four white-dressed men while my mother with tears was looking at my funeral procession from the second floor window and lamenting, "My child died, my child passed away." And my father was drinking alcohol in the dark living room to divert his sorrow.

When I awoke from my dream at midnight, as usual I needed to go to the toilet. Before I went out from my bed I said to myself, "Now, don't be afraid of monsters. They cannot kill my death. They are weaker than my death." And I could go to my work quite comfortably. But when I came back into my bed again, my dream was remembered and I could not distinguish whether it was a dream or real. Death became my greatest enemy, and nothing was more important for me than it. When my parents suggested going to the hospital to me, I furiously refused. "I would like to die at least between mother and father but not those cold, whitely dressed monsters!"

In those days I read a Buddhist fable which told me that if a child dies under twelve years old he will be able to go to heaven. Because in front of heaven and hell the Jizo Bodhisattva[1] is standing to help children to be sent to heaven. All human beings when they die must be blamed for the sins which they made in this world. The sins of adults are so numerous and severe that no one can atone for all of them. Therefore they must get the punishment in hell. But children make only a few, innocent sins. or amending the sins of children, Jizo Bodhisattva will help in front of heaven and hell.

When I read this fable I felt, "If that is so, I have no need to suffer about my death. It is rather a happy matter, I can go to heaven. But how sorrowful my parents and all adults are!" Then I pitied my parents who were worrying over my illness without knowing they must go to hell. I thought at least they have no need to worry over my death and illness. Those are welcome. And I was a very good child, working in the mountain, fishing for dinner in the river after school.

Why We Suffer 87

But it was when I became almost twelve years old that my worrying about death came alive again. My birth month was December, but around April of that year I tried to hurry my death. Otherwise the Jizo Bodhisattva would not help me at the world of death. In the night after my parents slept deeply, I tore open my pillow and ate the cotton inside. But I could not die. Then I tried to drink my urine to die. But after drinking a drop, my body threw it up.

And while I was looking for a good way to die, in the classroom of elementary school our teacher warned us not to eat unripened plums. He said, pointing to the rain outside of the windows, "In this rainy season if you eat an unripened plum you will get a terrible disease called intestinal typhoid, which is fatal." After the Second World War in this confused country, there were indeed many such infectious diseases. And my teacher, to make sure of our caution, guided us to one senior classroom and showed an empty desk and chair. He had worship for that empty seat and said to us, "This boy was healthy until a week ago. But he ate an unripened plum and was sent to the hospital for intestinal typhoid. Unfortunately he could not come home again but went to that other world." All classmates trembled with fear and determined not to touch any plums. But the inside of my mind jumped up with enjoyment.

As soon as school finished, I ran home, and before entering I went behind the house. In the rain, a fresh plum tree was serenely standing and many tiny plums were shining like green jewels. Quickly, but after making sure that no one was looking, I picked a few plums and put them into my mouth. They tasted purely sour but I ate. Though my teacher had said even one plum was enough for dying, I feared some misfortune so I ate three. And secretly I entered into my house and put in order all of my private possessions such as clothes, books, toys, and wrote a sentence to put in my drawer for my parents. It said, "thank you for your care about me, from now on I will take care of you from heaven." And I entered into my bed quietly.

When I awakened for supper I saw still the time was not coming for me, and the faces of parents seemed very clear, as if I were looking through a large magnifying glass. I thought they were worthy of being protected by me from heaven. When they worried even more about my health and my unusual calmness, I felt the more mercy for them. They seemed very charming though they were worrying so much.

The next day passed with the same clarity and calmness, and the next day also. When almost one week passed without anything happening, I suddenly was aware that I had been fooled by my teacher. I was not going to die at all, thought teachers unworthy of being trusted, and I suffered again over my death. I did not want to die after becoming twelve years old but I wanted to die before that birthday. Ceaselessly this contradictory problem of mine attacked me, but of course there were many times when I was forgetting about death, especially in the daytime.

In such a time my mother entered a hospital and my father went to a distant southern island to work. In the house old grandmother and three small children were left and oldest brother and sister went to a company. When I noticed that my birthday had passed over while I was busily working for daily life and school, it was already New Year's day. I was desperately sorry that I had missed the chance to enter into heaven, but I was somehow determined to solve the problem of death and instead of going to heaven, bring heaven to this world for adults also. Because I was beginning to be aware that even though only I go to heaven, if my mother and father and all other people don't go to heaven, what is there to being in heaven that is worth more than life as it is?

From that time I began to read thousands of books. I determined to read at least a book a day, without considering my reading ability and believing the proverb, "Reading a hundred times means naturally clear." Until I became nineteen years old I tried to seek the solution of death by reading books. I read about Confucianism, Taoism, Buddhism, Christianity, Eastern and Western philosophy, and many novels. Many people called me precocious and my reputation which spread beyond my native village made only needless problems for me. When I was fourteen I had begun reading in translation Nietzsche, Kierkegaard, Tolstoy, Dostoevsky, and so forth.

Of course I could not understand them very well. But when I

became nineteen years old I thought, "All great people are talking about death and love finally, and some books show that their authors are not knowing the solution yet, while some books are showing that the authors already know the answer. But even among those good books, still there is not the truth. They are only 'the finger pointing to show the moon.' " And that's why I decided to enter into the training monastery. And what I understood there is written in this book. I have almost no fear any more. I am almost perfectly happy.

Well, I am very sorry to talk so much about my private history. Only I wanted to give you some help for understanding the emptiness, called *Sunyata*. In the following chapter this emptiness will be explained more. But please know, if you really want to know the emptiness of Buddhism, the enlightenment of Bodhisattva Avalokitesvara, please train in my Zendo, Dokuso-kutsu, The Cave of Poison Grass. I will not withhold in the least the donation of the Dharma. Real study is the only way to get real enlightenment. Real understanding will become the daily practice. That means if we understand Hannya, we will be in the Dharma and will live in accord with Sila.

In my father's letter from Japan recently he wrote the following saying to me. He is already almost seventy years old.

> Every day is a good day for me even though I don't try to be so. Cleaning garden and inside house and looking at its sight while sitting a long time on the veranda makes for me a special enjoyment. Occasionally I will trim branches of the garden trees to help their natural growth. When I visited Dr. Asada, he said by measuring my blood pressure that I can die at any time. My blood pressure was higher than two hundred and fifty. Recently I was called to a mountain graveyard to chant the sutra for a burial service. While chanting I felt unbearable sufferings in my whole body. And as soon as I felt so I fainted, which was an extraordinary relief. It was a very hot day, especially for me, after being served a little alcohol at lunch and then climbing to the

mountain graveyard and chanting the sutra. Fortunately I came to myself and can see many things again. But I was enlightened that we have sufferings while we have our bodies, and when we say goodbye to the body, we have refreshing enjoyment. I think this will be said for the persons who die by motor car crash or any other death. They will feel tremendous suffering just before their death, but as soon as they separate from their bodies, they will be in the enjoyment. By the way, according to custom Zennists should write a stanza before death. But I think it is a cruel brutal thing to request so. Zennists can write the poem while they are living very well.[2] Anyway my hope is only that my sons and daughters and grandchildren live in good health and that others regardless of whether they have connection with me or not are living without fighting but peacefully.

Always my father writes very few sentences, but this letter was the longest one which I have received from him in all my life. Even if people about the same age as my father are still seeking many mortal things, what can they get? Instead of living such deluded lives, one time die and live freely, harmoniously. The life freed from suffering is the hopeful life for people. Such unawakened old men should have shame by reading this letter. If you don't deny one time completely, for you there is not your life.

風鳴不動天邊之月

日本國京都建云寺
文堂

V *Emptiness*

Understanding Cause and Effect (Sanskrit, *Hetu-phala*) is indispensable for understanding Sunyata correctly. The essence of the teaching of Mahayana Buddhism is Cause and Effect. Everything is changing in each moment in the phenomenal world. Therefore if we don't grasp the real being which is not a changeable mortal thing but eternal Law, truth, we cannot say we are really living. But there is no way to grasp the real being except through the phenomenal world. Therefore we should understand Cause and Effect to understand Sunyata.

The listener who received Sakyamuni Buddha's preaching of this Hannya Sutra was named Śāriputra. He was originally a Brahman teacher of one hundred people at Rajgir. When Sariputra was walking on a street, by chance he happened to talk with a disciple of Buddha, who told him, "All phenomena are arising from the Cause. My teacher preaches this Cause." These words dug into Sariputra's mind. For normal people this kind of saying has no more special meaning than the sound of wind from a horse. But for Sariputra, it was enough of an enlightened experience to become Buddha's disciple.

If you know the Cause you will know the Effect, because the Effect is also the name of the next Cause. In the Cause there is the inner, direct cause and the eternal, indirect cause. A grain of wheat is the direct cause, and water, soil, and so on are indirect causes for growing the wheat.

In modern society the improvement of the treatment of convicts is advocated loudly. But concern for the buildings, food, work, time, etc. of convicts is not yet part of the real improvement. Real improvement will begin when we realize the direct cause and the

Emptiness   93

indirect causes of crime. For the direct cause we human beings should all understand Sunyata, and for the indirect cause we human beings should all have responsibility. The crime of a convict is not only his crime but is our responsibility as well. I think even such wars as that now happening in Indo-China are happening because I am not working enough as a Buddhist priest.

Anyhow, there is Cause and Effect in this world. Therefore this world is the world of Sunyata. The reverse is also true.

Our Sakyamuni Buddha was thinking of the Cause of the mortality of human life when he got enlightenment. And he made a series of Twelve Steps: (1.) ignorance which is the origin of all delusions; (2.) volition which comes out of ignorance and leads to; (3.) consciousness which is the first mind at the time of conception; (4.) growth which is the mental activity and the growth of the body in the womb; (5.) the six organs which means possession of the six organs, eyes, ears, nose, tongue, body, and mind just at the time of going out from mother's womb; (6.) contact which is the stage around two to three years old, contact with many matters without distinguishing suffering and enjoyment; (7.) perception which means perceiving while distinguishing suffering and enjoyment, occurring from six or seven years old; (8.) love which is the stage, after fourteen or fifteen years old, of various desires, of seeking enjoyment and avoiding suffering; (9.) attachment which means being attached to desirable things; (10.) being which means living, and this makes the Effect of the future by means of love and attachment, leading to; (11.) birth; (12.) old age and death.

Among these, 1 and 2 are the Causes made in the past world, 3 through 7 are the Effects in the present world, 8 through 10 are the Causes made in the present world, and 11 and 12 are the Effects in the future world. This means each of the twelve steps is related in two ways, as Cause and as Effect, to the three worlds of past, present, and future. Sakyamuni Buddha observed this series of Twelve Steps from 1 to 12 and from 12 to 1 repeatedly in his meditation.

As you can see, in the above series all the world is being in mutual relationship and in the Law of Cause and Effect. Our beings depend on these, and that is why we should see the Sunyata. Otherwise we cannot be free from the suffering of the world of Cause and Effect and mutual relation while living by their power. Here we should know that everything is changing and whatever is, is only one time. Not only our life; in the same way all things are being only one time. In our life we cannot repeat anything. Whether it be suffering or happiness it comes only one time. From this, teachings such as "do your best in each moment" will appear, or many arts will be enjoyed. Without the feeling of this "only one time" or "only one," all arts will become very shallow. Not only the arts but all our lives as well will become very shallow.

In any case, if you understand the Law of Cause and Effect I can talk about the Sunyata. Sunyata denies the substance, contrary to the thought of Aristotle, Descartes, Spinoza, or Berkeley, but in agreement with Hume or Kant on this point.

For observing Sunyata, or Emptiness, there is the Analytical way and the Synthetic way. If the ways of observing it are different, naturally as a result the ways of practicing it will also differ. The first way is that of Hineyana Buddhists and the second of Mahayana Buddhists. Both ways were taught by Sakyamuni Buddha. Since the purpose of Buddhism is to help oneself and at the same time all others, we should understand and practice both ways. Without stomach there is no back, and without back there is no stomach. The relationship of Mahayana and Hineyana should, in my belief, be understood in this way. For convenience in explaining Sunyata, however, I will divide Buddhism in two here.

Generally Hineyana says that all beings of this world arise by Cause and Effect, or Karma, and when this karma disappears all beings also break up to return to the original Dharma itself. All beings will be born and will die.[1] Consequently Hineyana thinks, first, that human life is mortal and its teaching is to let us know the mortality. Second, Hineyana says that human life is suffering, the so-called four or eight sufferings which I have explained. The suffering of death is the largest and the solution of death is the most important work of the priest to the people. Without understanding death, people cannot live freely, correctly.

Emptiness

In the late nineteenth century a great Japanese general, Saigo, also said, "Unless a person doesn't care about name, money, women, . . . death, he is not able to do any great work." However, if I understand in the Mahayana way, this saying means: without solving these, and graduating from these, we cannot do any great work.

According to Hineyana the suffering of life is our normal state. Everything which we receive from outside is suffering: the suffering of receiving suffering, the suffering of receiving enjoyment, and the suffering of receiving not-suffering and not-enjoyment. You can see easily the suffering of receiving suffering. If you receive one suffering, others will appear like the links of a chain. It is like the saying, "on the crying face, a bee attacks," or, "misfortunes seldom come alone." And indeed how often we can see the case of a poor family getting illness, the parents dying, and on top of that a child will die. . . .

The suffering of receiving enjoyment was called so because while we are enjoying receiving enjoyment it is enjoyment, but sooner or later it turns to suffering. Drinking alcohol as one likes is enjoyment but it makes the alcoholic, or the cause of family dispute, or illness, etc. It is a very ironic fact, though such an extreme case does not happen, that if a wife cooks very good meals, husband or children become as fat as hippopotamuses and they cannot then have any gratitude to wife or mother.

This reminds me of the novel *Jean Christophe* by Romain Rolland. The chief character Christophe did not like to go to the concert hall when he was a child because it was intolerable suffering for him to go out from the hall after the exquisite enjoyment of music. At least, while we don't have inner enjoyment we should feel so. When you have a baby you should know you made the cause for the suffering of separation from him. Therefore a person who is excited by some enjoyment is, for me, untrustable for his own life and for others' also. Real enjoyment or enlightenment is not the kind of abnormal psychology described in some books about Zen. People cannot see any difference between enlightenment and the drunkeness by L.S.D. Real enjoyment is while crying in the cold snowfall, smiling, and while smiling at the warm fireside, crying. Such is humanity; not God, not beast. Why is the Mona Lisa so great? "Even the sound of blowing your nose is the fragrance of plum blossoms."

The sufferings of receiving not-suffering and not-enjoyment means that while we are living vacantly without suffering or enjoyment, our life is passing away, becoming old, coming close to death. Then, receiving neither suffering nor enjoyment finally makes only suffering. In this way Hineyana will observe human life as full of sufferings.

Third, Hineyana says that all our lives are dirty, just as even the most beautiful woman makes urine and excrement. From her eyes, nose, ears, mouth, and all her skin dirt is produced. The human body is already a source of pollution. If Dostoevsky's Alyosha marries, he will be disappointed by his wife. Of course, not only women, but men also, all our forms are dirty.

In Thailand I needed to shave my head, underarm hair and eyebrows for this reason. When I pointed below my abdomen and asked whether I should also shave or not, they smiled and said it was not necessary. Generally they dislike the color black even more than white people do. That is a reason why they will wear yellow robes. Thailand priests are insisting on Hineyana in this matter. Anyway, in all these observations of life Hineyana is concluding that this world is a dirty, hateful world.

But the thankful thought of Sakyamuni Buddha begins from this point, for he said we have such mortal, suffering, and dirty lives because of the effects of our karma and klesa (delusions) which were made by us in the past world. Therefore we should cut off the Cause of these Effects, cut off the karma and klesa by the Analytical way to observe the Sunyata and be free from all sufferings in order to live very well as Bodhisattvas. The Analytical way to observe Sunyata means, literally, to analyze all Dharmas and discover the universal validity, Sunyata; that is, to realize all phenomena are the mortal harmony of the Five Skandhas by the Law of Cause and Effect, mutual relation, and have not any ultimate existence or substance. Moreover, Sunyata is not a thing to be invented but to be discovered, as was done by Sakyamuni Buddha.

For instance, even a house is the momentary harmony of such materials as boards, bricks, iron, paint, etc. No one can say a piece of board is the substance of the house. Therefore in the house there is no substance. Rather, the house is only a mortal harmony. Even a board has no substance; it is the harmony of water, fiber, and so on. Observing the emptiness of substance and the being of harmony in this way is observing Sunyata Analytically. Naturally all sufferings are also empty and you will be free from them.

Another way to observe Sunyata is the Synthetic way. It can be understood if you know Mahayana which, like Hineyana, says that all beings of the world arose by one's karma and Cause and Effect. But Mahayana says that the substance of one's karma and Cause and Effect themselves are empty because all Dharmas are empty from the beginning, and that in the freedom of Sunyata there is the birth and death of phenomena. This is very different from Hineyana. Hineyana still sees birth and death as actually existing in the Cause and Effect.

Second, Mahayana takes the long view that human life is enjoyment. The matter of fact that life is suffering is the same for both Hineyana and Mahayana, and for all other religions. But here is the reason why Mahayana will understand Cause and Effect optimistically. By the Cause we are getting the suffering of the Effect. If that is so, receiving suffering must be enjoyable for us. The reason is that by receiving, we are paying back all debts of sufferings which were made in all past time. It is just like owing money which is a very painful matter, but if by having suffering we can pay back all debts it is a very enjoyable thing. Then while receiving suffering, paying back our debt is great enjoyment. Furthermore, Mahayana believes we were originally all Buddhas, but now we are not Buddhas because of our karma and ignorant desires. But if that is so, receiving sufferings as ignorant sentient beings is the process to become Buddha. And this process is a very enjoyable thing which is no different from the enjoyment of perfected purpose while we live as trainers of Bodhisattvahood to attain Buddhahood. From this kind of understanding of the Cause and Effect of life, the following sayings were spoken: "Receiving sufferings with enjoyment is the study to become Buddha," or, "For the trainer of the Way, there is no suffering," or, "Every day is a good day."

Enlightenment means the dynamic, harmonious life built on the contradiction of suffering and enjoyment. Naturally enlightenment cannot be attained by living in the pure enjoyment or by living as a holy saint. On the cross of contradiction, make empty all beings and let humanity arise as is its nature to do so. Then certainly all contradictions will become the harmonious contrast, such as is expressed by the Zen phrase, "Willows are green, flowers are red," or "Eyes are horizontal, nose is vertical."

Though Hineyana sees life as dirty, Mahayana sees life as pure. Pollution from the holes of the human body is dirty indeed when we see them only, but they are all part of the wonderful activity of Buddha. This world is including all contrasts such as purity and dirtiness, beauty and ugliness, good and bad, comfort and discomfort, and so on. This world is absolutely self-contradictory, and at one time the self-unified world which is heaven, pure land.

All the above differences between the views of life and the world held by Hineyana and Mahayana came from their different understanding of Sunyata. Hineyana begins by affirming the being of all Dharmas and then denies them by analyzing each of them. But Mahayana will deny the beings of all Dharmas from the beginning and say that all of the phenomenal world, like a shadow, exists because of our delusion. Then the Mahayana way to observe Sunyata is called the Synthetic way. It will not analyze the house as the harmony of boards, bricks, and paint, but will see it as emptiness itself. If you see Sunyata this way, you can live in the understanding that "form is formless form" or "klesa is Bodhi," "ignorant sentient beings are Buddha," "the difference is the sameness," or "world is I," "zero is one, and one is all other numbers." What is one? This pen is one, I am also one, my house is also one. America is one, too. The world is also one. The universe is one. If everything can be called one, what is the real one in the meaning of one? Is one only the name of the limited idea of beings in our discrimination? How can you make two by one plus one while you don't know one? If you understand Sunyata, understanding zero is easy and zero is all. But one and from one to two will not be understood from my words or from studying with your dualistic discrimination. Unfortunately you cannot really understand the Sunyata of Mahayana without real training under a correct teacher. Sunyata not only means to enter into the emptiness but means also coming back from the emptiness. It is not only to make empty everything but to be alive to everything, as in the Zen words, "The blossom of iron tree." If you understand the Sunyata of Mahayana you can help many other people, not only yourself. Hineyana is only for helping yourself. Related to this point is a koan from *Hekigan-roku*, Case Forty:

> An official assistant, Rikko, said by way of talking with Zenji Nansen, "Rev. Jo said that the Universe and I have the same root; all things and I are one body. How surprising a saying it is!" Nansen pointed to a peony in the front garden to show to Rikko. And he said, "Social people see this peony as if they are in a dream."

Always religion has its Sila, which is the practice of its thought and teaching. Like the official assistant Rikko in this koan, if we have such beautiful, formal dress of thought or discrimination we cannot practice freely. Even though it be gold, if it enters into our eyes it makes only trouble for us. Beethoven said, "There is no rule which for the cause of more beauty cannot be destroyed." Anyway, finally it depends on how much we really understand Sunyata.

The philosophical or rational understanding of Sunyata was perfected by Sakyamuni Buddha in India. But the understanding of Sunyata which was practical, testified with our body, was developed in China under the name of Mu (pronounced Wu, in Chinese) by Zen Buddhists. And this development was taken further in Japan, especially by Zenji Hakuin and his inheritors.

In my thinking, it is very natural history that one aspect of Sunyata, truth itself, like a river, will not change; but the other aspect, the usages or works of Sunyata, will or should change like a river's water. My great hope is that this development of the usages or works will be accomplished by people of the West, notably Americans with their great energy and love for the human world. Generally people of the East do not cherish the treasures they already have, as a result of their particular thirst for Western culture in these past hundred years or so. Eastern people absorbed themselves into cultivating the mind, and as a result they are still very poor about their bodies. For this reason they are longing too much for bodily things while throwing away the care of their mind. And in comparison, the opposite can be said for Western people who have had the poorness of mind and richness of body. Then, I feel, in Eastern Ocean there were a lot of fish which can be seen scarcely now through the covering oil. In Western Desert there was a lot of sand, and now through the blowing dust a few plants can be seen.

We cannot divide mind and body. That was the ceaseless declaration of the people of Zen Buddhism. Mu is no different in its philosophical idea from Sunyata. But about understanding and practically living, Mu and Sunyata are very different. In *The Sayings of Zenji Joshu Shinzai*[2] there is the following story:

A monk asked to Zenji Joshu, "Is there Buddha nature in a dog or not?"

"U" ("Yes, there is"), Zenji Joshu replied.

"If that is so, why is it packed into such a skin?" the monk asked again.

"It is doing so, knowingly," replied the Zenji.

On another occasion another monk asked to Zenji Joshu, "Is there Buddha nature in a dog or not?"

"Mu" ("No, there is not"), came the reply.

"All sentient beings have their Buddha nature, why is there not for the dog?"

"Because of the karma of the dog," replied the Zenji.

Buddha nature in the above stories means the truth which is not to be grasped by recognition, judgment, and proposition, but as the whole of beings, universe, Dharmas. Sakyamuni Buddha declared in the *Nirvana Sutra*, "All sentient beings have their Buddha nature."

Without this Buddha nature there is no reason we can awaken for the Buddha nature. Therefore if we train we can enlighten.

In the first part of the above story the monk was thinking that in a dirty dog there should not be such Buddha nature because Buddha nature is a wonderful beautiful thing. And in the second part of the story, the monk was thinking that according to the sutra, Buddha nature should be in everything, even a humble dog. The problem was that both of these monks understood quite well about Buddha-nature or truth or Sunyata, but only in their half-perfected discrimination and not by their whole mind and body.

Then as a teacher, Joshu encouraged the monks by saying freely "U" or "Mu." His mind was, 'You want to know really about Buddha nature, Sunyata. Your will to know is very good, but it is a sorrowful matter that you are trying to understand this with only your brain, not by your body. But you should realize our discrimination cannot understand the emptiness, Sunyata. It should be understood by the emptiness itself. Try to be empty. It is the only way to enlighten for the Sunyata.'

Naturally "U" or "Mu" do not mean, respectively, "there is, being," or "there is not, nothingness." Rather they both mean, "not that," "not yet" for the trainers until they really live in the Sunyata as Sunyata. The story of the dog was deepened by priest Mumon Ekai who got enlightenment by this koan after six years of hard training. Priest Mumon promoted the understanding of this Mu, or Sunyata, by becoming itself, which means penetrating to our original nature itself. And he settled this koan as the first border which all trainers should go through, arranging it as the first case in his collection, *Mumon-Kan*. This is what he said about Mu:

> For the practical study of Zen, at first you should pass through the border which was set up by Zen Patriarchs. To reach the exquisite enlightenment, you should empty all that which is normally called mind and consciousness. If you don't experience physically emptying the consciousness, your life is like the ghosts who are depending on grasses or trees. Well, tell me what is the

border of the Patriarchs? . . . This one letter Mu is the first border to the essence of religion. It will be named "The Gateless Border of the Zen Sect." If there is a person who can pass through the border, not only is he able to meet with Joshu, but he can walk hand in hand with all historical Patriarchs intimately, and under the same eyebrows he can see with the same eyes, he can hear with the same ears. Is that not the really wonderful life? Then all of you, why don't you pass through this border? For that become a lump of doubt with all of your heart and body, which is said to have three hundred and sixty bones and joints and eighty-four thousand pores, and concentrate to this Mu. Try to solve this every day and night. But don't understand this Mu as such empty emptiness as Taoism, or as relative "Mu" as opposed to "u". It should be like swallowing the hot iron ball, your trying to solve this Mu; you cannot throw it up but also cannot swallow it. Wash out from yourself all former useless prejudiced discrimination and understanding in this way. And if you continue a long time, naturally the difference of outside and inside will disappear to become Mu itself. This experience is like the dream of a dumb person who cannot tell to others; you know only by yourself. The actions which burst from such an experience surprise heaven and shake hell, and you are just like the one who snatches the great sword from General Kan-u. And you can kill Buddha when you meet with him, can kill the Patriarch when you face with him, can be in the perfect freedom on the cliff of death-life and can live freely anywhere, throughout the transmigration of the six worlds and the four kinds of birth, as if you are purely playing. Then how should you concentrate to this Mu? Try with all the power you possess to this Mu. If you don't rest but continue ceaselessly, the light of Dharma will be turned on in your mind. Saying in the stanza:

> Dog—Buddha nature!
> The supreme Law was shown,
> Falling even a bit into the relative u and mu
> Destroys your body to death.

A thankful thing is Mumon's insatiate encouragement to train, given with love more than the love from one's real father. He knew entirely through his experience that love is not to comfort the suffering one to let him live in the status quo, but to cut off the cause of sufferings. Without training in the Bodhisattva Way, no one can get real satisfaction and the unspeakable enjoyment of human life. "The longest way round is the shortest way home." To understand Sunyata, he taught to concentrate for one's original nature through the meditation of Mu. If we do not awaken for our original nature, the Sunyata in us will not have creative work such that we can go beyond Sakyamuni Buddha or the Patriarchs. How unfree to carry the house of golden tradition as if we were snails. Life, proved against death, can live after destroying the old shells. For instance, if the Japanese don't deny being Japanese one time, they cannot live as Japanese in the world anymore. How can we deny ourselves completely? To enter the burning fire of the correct teacher is the best way to train highly the formless sword.

Here I will show you how the Japanese Zennist will master this koan Mu since the time of Zenji Hakuin (1685–1768), who is considered the restorer of Rinzai Zen in Japan. His greatness will be understood even by seeing just the following questions on Mu which were set up by him and later arranged in the poem "The Song of *Mu*" (*Muji-no-uta*) by Zenji Kosen Imakita (1826–1892). I will translate "The Song of *Mu*" here without any explanation, because as you know already, the letters about koans are dead things while you don't become Mu and until Mu itself also disappears.

The Song of *Mu*

You should study this matter really in detail,
Don't do roughly, you will slip off.
Without comprehending the profound meaning of the Dharma,
Having a guessed view, resigned with worldly wisdom,
By licking the slaver of the teacher who is like an old woman,
Unloading the heavy burden while thinking you have enlightened,
All makes you haughty and full of much extreme pride.

Don't stop on the way before truly cutting the seeds of death-life,
Made in innumerable kalpas past.
How terrible the first step is!

All students of real training,
You had better get complete enlightenment,
I beg to you, like penetrating through
The base and the aureole of Buddha, indeed,
Train your raw iron in the furnace
A thousand, million times and in addition to that,
Polish sharply the iron by the examination of *Mu*,
And your daily practice should be
Suitable for your comprehension,
With varied practical experiences, freely.
Such a great sword makes one cringe even by a glance,
Also can cut easily the verbally expressed, hard-to-pass koans.
How trustworthy in the future your training!
About *Mu*: this one letter border
Was admired of old by wise trainers also.
Originally this was chanted only as *Mu*
By Joshu, who trained on the training
By pilgrimaging until eighty years old,
Having enlightened at age eighteen,
Like destroying the house and spreading the family.
This is the profound, wonderful one word.

Though there are many people who know the dead phrase,
There is hardly a person who comprehends the living phrase;
The untransmittable key is in the living phrase.
Even if you know the forms, they are all dead phrases.
The one who misleads the trainers
Is named a corrupter for his double tongue;
The punishment should be seen soon.
The secret key of the transmission from heir to heir
Is not to be gotten by easy grasping.

Emptiness 105

The most important thing is to pass this *Mu*.
The crossroads of evil and truth will become bright with this.
On this point a severe teacher of our sect will have responsibility.

If you see *Mu*, show me proof.
Tell me the phrase of transcended death-life.
Before the monk had yet asked about Buddha-nature
And before Joshu replied *Mu*,
What is your viewpoint?
Look at it after your death, after cremation of the remains.
Still I ask you
To pick up *Mu* a little,
You should see the figure of *Mu*.
Show me the origin, the root of *Mu*.
Use *Mu* freely and easily,
Use it lightly but freely.
Divide *Mu* to minute pieces.
There are still the more interesting examinations:
Without saying *Mu* how will you say?
You also should read clearly, distinctly
The stanza of twenty *Mu* letters, written by Priest Mumon.
In the stanza of Goso, the first two phrases are rather shallow,
But the third and fourth are deep;
You ought to catch the guts
Of Zenji Chuko completely, perfectly.
And answer sometimes as *U*.
This also is important, don't lose yourself.
And by the greeting of Karma also
Don't be defeated, don't be pulled down.
And after you are through, train until
You can see the answer for "as knowing, commit."
Distinguish *Mu* and Karma,
You should see the great distance between them also.
In addition, in four ways
You should express,

THE CAVE OF POISON GRASS

This is such a high examination that
You can't pass easily, will get sick.
Please pass through each of these.

Always training in Dhyana is important.
From Dhyana bring out Prajna,
And make your own
The true understanding and the works of *Mu*.
After clarifying the words *Mu* and Karma,
Train on the training and
Make the stanza freely
For the true understanding and the works of *Mu*.
And after enlightening, make the stanza happily
For the true meaning of these four,
Mu, Karma, U, and *as knowing, commit*.
There are many branches and leaves
For the examinations of *Mu* which I roughly wrote.

You can say a little that you saw
Mu after finishing those examinations.
That you should be discreet is the first step,
The thing to fear is easily going through,
Don't ever say you finished *Mu*
While there is even a bit of hanging doubt.
After passing the difficult-to-pass and difficult-to-solve koans,
Still there are heavy thick mountain borders.
Pass all of these remaining ones
Which were called "behind the mountain of *Mu*."

Use your body as the foundation with tears of blood, and know
The burnt-tailed fish becomes the dragon
After passing through the difficult cascades
Of three dragon gates with pain and hard work.
Indeed it is hopeless that this matter
Will be passed by the ordinary man.

The teacher who certifies easily
Seems very poor in his hand.
There are such teachers who fool one with appearance,
In accord with the ending and frivolous world.
On this point you should have an eye when you tour.
Don't be taken in by the gathering of multitudes,
Don't be deceived by the purple or yellow robes.
Have the spirit of the true Man, and
Keep the tradition of the Patriarchs' way of tour,
The austere, frank, high, alone, and precipitous way.
Please be careful, all you great ones.
If you do so the time will come
When you can recompense at once the obligation to Buddha,
The obligation to teacher and parents.
How wonderful, how interesting! My mates of the same subject!
Not speaking about it is the secretness,
Not talking is the profound Way.

VI X ≧ Y

My Sariputra, form is no different from emptiness is no different from form; form is emptiness as itself, and emptiness is form as itself. The same can be said of sensation, thought, volition, and consciousness.

Sha ri shi, shiki fu i ku, ku fu i shiki, shiki soku ze ku, ku soku ze shiki. Ju so gyo shiki yaku bu nyo ze.

Sariputra is one of the ten great disciples of Sakyamuni Buddha.[1] The ten great disciples are:

1. Sariputra, unsurpassed in wisdom,
2. Maudgalyāyana, unsurpassed in supernatural powers,
3. Mahā-kāśyapa,[2] unsurpassed in humanity,
4. Aniruddha, unsurpassed in seeing with the eye of Heaven,
5. Subhadra, unsurpassed in understanding Sunyata,
6. Pūrṇa-maitrāyaṇī-putra, unsurpassed in preaching the teachings,
7. Kātyāyana, unsurpassed in discussion of the truth,
8. Upāli, unsurpassed in keeping and knowing the precepts,
9. Rāhula,[3] unsurpassed in practicing and knowing the details of the precepts,
10. Ānanda, unsurpassed in memory of the teachings.

Sakyamuni Buddha had disciples of greatly varied characteristics, like these ten people. Among them, Sariputra was the most suitable person to hear the preaching of the Hannya Sutra. Then, in this sutra, he became the listener. Sakyamuni Buddha talked to him very kindly. As you read this short sutra, you see Sakyamuni Buddha calling him twice by name, saying, "My Sariputra."

Śāri means "spring nightingale" and *putra* means "child." Then Sariputra means a child of the beautiful mother who is like a spring nightingale. A Japanese priest, Rev. Godo Nakanishi who is famous for his love and research of the wild birds, described a kind of Japanese nightingale in one of his books.[4] Though I don't know that Sari is exactly this kind of Japanese nightingale, the following excerpt from his book will be useful for understanding the Sari:

> A nightingale is crying purely
> In the field of bamboo grasses on the mountain top,
> Though the weather makes shine or shadow there.

This poem was made by Rigen Kinoshita at the top of Rokko Mountain, if my memory is correct. This excellent singer who nests in the bamboo grasses or in the miscanthus field is a bird of the highland in summer. If this bird had not been domesticated since old times, the calm, significant sound "Ho-Hokekyo" would have stopped the feet of numerous people with its dignity, gentleness, and skillfulness. It has a horizontally tapering profile and sharply standing tail, a thin bill and a quick motion which have different charms from those of the bunting family. Really this bird's note which has no crack makes an enjoyable and comfortable place out of the rather monotonous sun-shining miscanthus field without any flower. I will stretch out my legs and light my pipe. I will lie down, turning my face upward. Insects of the mountain will crawl up on my pants or anywhere else without fear because my body is too large to be feared by them. In such a time if I find the gregarious wild flowers around me, the sound of the nightingale becomes much too wonderful a thing, like the song of the ceremonial festival of the highlands.

So, as is to be expected, the mother of Sariputra was a beautiful and a good person. On this occasion, if I talk of the greatness of mother and father, I will say they are like Hannya itself, which has both wisdom and love to children. Since the beginningless beginning of the world, if there has been no parents there would have been no beings in this world. Of course there would not have been any plants, animals and human beings also.

Sunyata is the beginningless beginning of the world which has two aspects: wisdom, which is emptiness, and love, which is form. Emptiness tells us the sameness, and form tells us the difference. The sameness sees the substance of all forms. Then it can be said that a mountain is not different from an ocean, mountain is ocean; or man is not different from woman, the man is the woman. Their value is not different, both are the same. And as humanity, woman and man, the old and the young, the poor and the rich, the wise and the foolish, and all such contrasting individuals do not differ; every one has the same respectable value.

The difference sees the forms of the substance. Then it can be said that mountain is mountain and ocean is ocean, or man is man and woman is woman; the man has a different value from the woman, the woman has a different value from the man. And as humanity, woman and man, the old and the young, the poor and the rich, the clever and the foolish, and all such contrasting individuals have not the same but their own respectable value. Humanity is the name of the substance and its works, of emptiness and form. Humanity is included in Sunyata.

People don't understand these two aspects; sameness and difference very well because they cannot understand this Sunyata very well. And they will insist on only one side. For instance, sleeping with another man's wife while saying that everything is empty and the same, or seeking the same dress, work, or position as the opposite sex, is not seeing the aspect of difference. And using woman as if she were a slave of man or seeking some special thing too much means not seeing the sameness.

Then for understanding Sunyata, difference and sameness, if we think of our parents it will help us very much. Because a mother has a great part of seeing the difference, love to child, and a father has a great part of seeing the sameness, wisdom to child.

Our ideal situation as human beings is having a family with both parents and children. Father will scold the child and mother will be sorry for the child. The good father must scold the child when the child will not see the sameness. And the good mother must comfort the child when the child will not see the difference. In modern society gradually such good parents are disappearing and consequently good human children are disappearing. How sorrowful a matter it is for me that no one understand Sunyata!

In the *Diamond Prajna Sutra*,[5] this phrase was meant for such good parents: "Indeed there is no place to stay but it makes arise the mind." A Japanese Bodhisattva, Gyoki,[6] made a poem:

> By hearing the sound of mountain birds
> Ho-ro, ho-ro,
> I think of them as my mother, as my father.

For all human children, parents are necessary. Think a moment about your mother. She protected you in her womb at first, she had great suffering to deliver you, she forgot her life itself to nurse you, she nursed you with her own life, milk, she chewed hard foods and gave them to you through her mouth, she gave you the dried part of her bed after you made it wet, she washed all of your dirt, she needed to do bad things for her karma and the world to help you. Even though you are separated from her in the far place, still she thinks about your life and she will love you eternally. And father gave to you birth, taught the correctness or truth and provided to you for growth, he gave you a safe place, showed you the serenity. There is no end to recounting all of their greatness.[7]

Mother is always worrying, as in this old Japanese poem:

> Where are you now?
> In this cold weather,
> My silly, my foolish child!

THE CAVE OF POISON GRASS

Or even if you die, still she thinks of you, like the nun, Reverend Chiyo in her poem:

> How far may my child go today,
> Chasing the dragonfly in the field?

But generally when you notice the greatness of your parents, already they are gone. You will remember them, like the poet Issa in his poem:

> What lonely coldness this
> My lazy sleeping in the daytime
> Without anyone who scolds me!

In some unfortunate case you may say you did not get such great love and wisdom from your parents. Really there is no such case, even if you were thrown at birth into a trash can by them. But meanwhile if I agree with your poor thinking about your parents, I should say to you that if that is true, therefore you should love your wife or husband and your child to make good cause for the future. And try to understand a koan from *Hekigan-roku,* Case Sixteen:

> A monk asked to Zenji Kyosei, "I will peck the shell from the inside, and you, please urge the shell from the outside."
> Kyosei asked, "But are you living or not?"
> The monk replied, "Why not? If I am not living, I will be shamed by social people."
> Kyosei said, "You are the one who is living in the wild grasses."

In any case, we should have gratitude for parents more and more. And also we should have gratitude for our children more and more. If there is no child we cannot understand such greatness of parents. That's the first reason why we should have gratitude to our child. A child makes us recognize the importance of the sameness and the difference.

Even though I have talked of all the above matters, still I fear people don't understand very well and don't practice at all as Bodhisattvas. Therefore I would dare say further, "Emptiness is no different from form." This was said to guard against understanding only one side of the truth by thinking that everything is empty, sameness. And all the following words are said for making your understanding completely sure.

The waves have thousands of differences but all of them are water. Water is water but it has thousands of forms. There are five fingers and each of them is different while all are only one hand. Water, or hand, or all things are different in form but all of them are the same one, emptiness.

Still further let me explain about the relationship of emptiness and form. Emptiness means absoluteness, and form means relativity. The Hannya Sutra is telling us that relativity is absoluteness. But it is difficult to explain this because when we say absoluteness, it is not absoluteness anymore. It was thought by us, which means it is relativity. Therefore we cannot say absoluteness = relativity, $x = y$. Absoluteness must always be larger than relativity, $x > y$. Otherwise we are talking about absoluteness as relativity. Absoluteness is always beyond our relativity. But relativity should be larger than absoluteness. Because if relativity were exactly the same as absoluteness, no works could come as the act of absoluteness. Therefore we cannot say that relativity = absoluteness, or $y = x$. But we should say $y > x$. Then the relationship of absoluteness to relativity will become the relation $x \gtreqless y$. But still the Hannya Sutra tells that $x = y$, $y = x$. On this point with our thought we cannot understand $x \gtreqless y$. Then since the beginning of the world the physical experience of the truth has been emphasized. Beyond our logic there is the religious life. On this point many people think religion is a kind of mysticism. Certainly religion is mysticism for ignorant people. But for the enlightened person it is naturalism.

Anyway, if we understand "form is no different from emptiness, emptiness is no different from form," we can live freely even in any kind of suffering. Buddhism is the Middle Way. This Middle Way does not mean the middle in time or place. It means not both edges. We will not make the wall of time and place. Then the Middle Way means being free from any time and place, Sunyata. In *The Sixth Patriarch's Sutra*[8] written by Tokui, there is the following story:

One day the Fifth Patriarch, Gunin (601-674), said to all his seven hundred disciples, "The problem of the death-life is the most important thing. Understanding our original nature which is Prajna is the way to solve the problem. Now each of you make a stanza and let me see it. If one of you is understanding Prajna I will give him the Dhrama of Transmission."

There was the Head Monk, Jinshu (605?-706), who was getting great respect from all monks. The seven hundred monks decided not to make any stanza, thinking, "The Head Monk, Jinshu, is the one who is suitable to inherit the Dharma Transmission. Even if we made stanzas, they will make only trouble for Teacher Gunin."

Jinshu felt very much responsibility for his followers' respect and expectation. But he did not want to make the stanza for becoming the heir. He thought that seeking the Law is good, but seeking to become heir is unclean, like the normal man's mind. But without writing the stanza he could not get the Law either.

Finally after a lot of thinking, he determined to write his stanza on the wall of a corridor in the night. It read:

> Our body is like the Bodhi-tree,
> Our mind is like the bright mirror-stand.
> Let us clean all the time and
> Not let any dust gather upon us.

And he thought, "In the morning Teacher Gunin will see this. If the Teacher thinks it is good, I will have worship to him; if the Teacher thinks it is not enough, I will continue to train."

The next day the Fifty Patriarch Gunin saw this stanza and thought, "Not perfect yet." But he thought it was better than any kind of religious picture on the wall. And although he was employing a painter to make illustrations from a sutra, he stopped him and said to all monks.

"If you chant this stanza, you will not fall into the devil way, can get enlightenment."

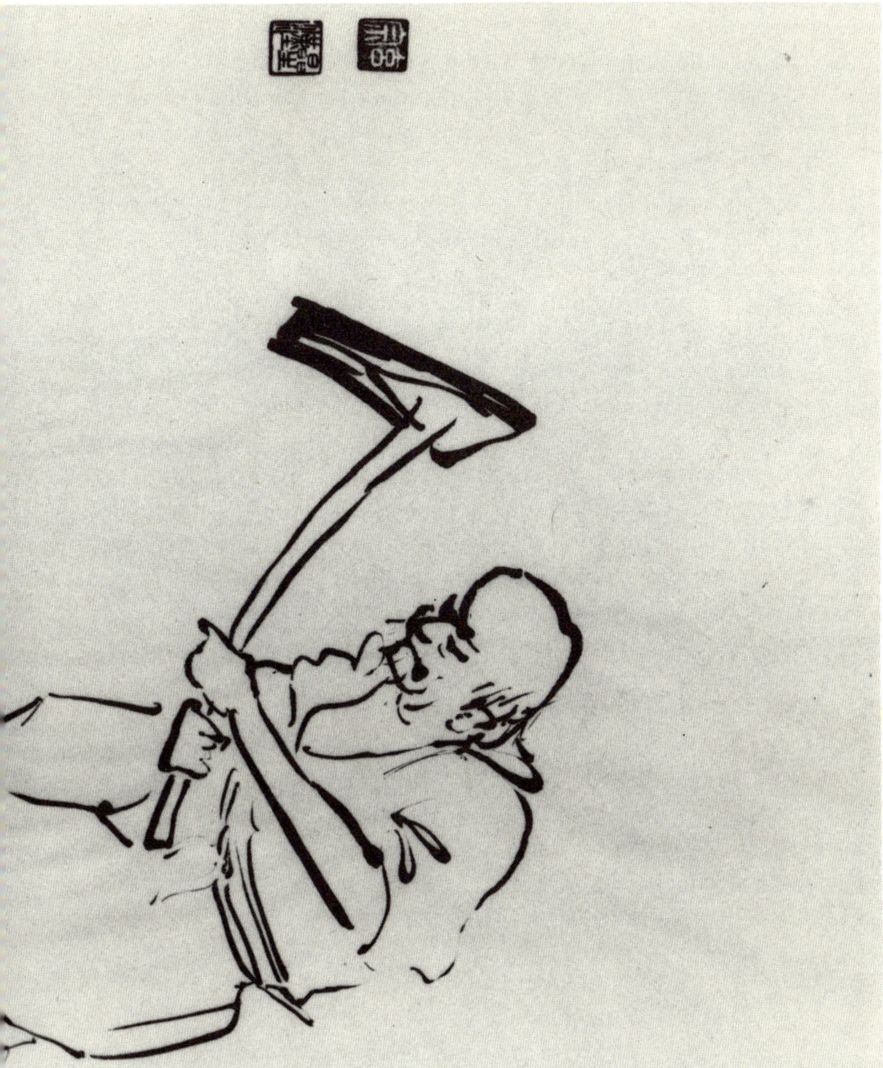

And he called Jinshu in the night and said to him, "You should know inside of the gate, not only outside. You should see more your original nature, which is not-to-be-born, not-to-die. Try to make another stanza."

There was Eno (639-713) who was still a fresh person in the monastery and not yet a monk. He was working in back of the temple pounding rice. But he heard a lay trainer chanting Jinshu's stanza. Eno asked this lay trainer about the stanza.

The lay trainer told him, "Don't you know? This stanza was made by the Head Monk, Jinshu. Our Teacher Gunin announced to all monks to make a stanza for inheriting the Dharma Transmission." Eno asked the lay trainer to bring him to the wall to have worship for the stanza of Jinshu. Standing in front of the wall upon which the stanza was written, Eno, who had not studied, could not read the letters. There was a person, Nichiyo, who could read for him. After hearing the stanza, Eno said, "I also have one stanza. Can you write for me?"

Nichiyo was surprised, but Eno said, "Don't insult the fresh trainer. In the people of lower class there is very high wisdom sometimes, and so often there is no wisdom in the people of high class. If you insult the fresh trainer you will get endless, limitless punishment."

Nichiyo said, "All right, let me write your stanza. But don't forget, if you get the Law, you should help me."

The stanza was written:

> First of all, Bodhi has no tree,
> Bright mirror has no stand.
> Originally there is not a thing,
> Where can we gather the dust?

Many people think the stanza of Jinshu is not yet showing the enlightened world, and that Eno's stanza is better. But I don't think so. Both are expressing the same thing, but from opposite sides. Jinshu is saying, "emptiness is form," and Eno "form is emptiness."

Then for Prajna, Sunyata, both are needed. In historical fact, the Fifth Patriarch transmitted the Dharma to both Jinshu and Eno.

Sakyamuni Buddha got enlightenment under the Bodhi-tree. Jinshu is saying in his stanza that we have no need to choose such a special place and time because our body itself is the Bodhi-tree. Wherever we are, we are under the Bodhi-tree. Buddha got enlightened eye which can see everything as suchness without any cloud of ego. It is just like a bright mirror which will not make any more beauty even when a good person stands in front of it, and will not make less beauty even when a bad person stands in front of it. The bright mirror will reflect any kind of object as suchness very fairly without any exception. Then Jinshu said our mind is like that bright mirror. We are originally pure. But while we are living, we will forget this Bodhi and mirror, and we will be deceived by their dust. Into the pure Bodhi and mirror all forms enter, and while we are human beings we will be affected by these forms. It is just like a man who tries to get a beautiful woman while knowing the beautiful woman is also the mortal, changing, momentary form. She is only such a harmonious form but has not any substance.

Then naturally we should clean all these dusts, should not let them gather on our free, pure, eternal Bodhi and mirror. Jinshu said very well that emptiness is form. But Eno said that even such Bodhi or mirror or all other dusts are empty. There is not any substance in the Bodhi or mirror or dust; naturally we cannot even dream of bringing any dust anywhere from any place. He is telling that form is emptiness. Both Jinshu and Eno are of course each telling complementary sides in their stanzas. Therefore I will say that both are needed for Prajna, Sunyata. If you see these, you will understand emptiness is not simply form as in normal mathematics. It is more than $x = y$, or $y = x$. Without religious experience under a correct teacher you cannot understand $x \gtreqless y$.

If you understand this Sunyata, you have no need to train only for yourself anymore, but you should train for all others. Without understanding Sunyata, even if you want to live for others, how can you? Can you really help others without understanding this?

VII Inviolable Being

My Sariputra, this empty form of all Dharmas can not be born and not be ruined, not be polluted and not be purified, and not be increased and not be decreased.

Sha ri shi, ze sho ho ku so, fu sho fu metsu, fu ku fu jo, fu zo fu gen.

Here the Sutra goes on to tell us the character of Sunyata, which is not simple empty emptiness. Therefore it is called "empty form" instead of "emptiness." "All Dharmas" means "all forms." The character of Sunyata will be understood and testified by your life if you practice the Six Paramitas as a Bodhisattva. To understand it simply should be easy for modern people thanks to the development of scientific theories such as the Laws of the Conservation of Energy and Matter.

But the problem is that people cannot live by testifying with their practical lives. Because they always see the limited, momentary part of the phenomena and will say, "Even though there is Prajna or Sunyata or 'not be born' and 'not be ruined', still in fact we must die and we were born." And in the end they will complain about abstract, incompetent religion and will say, "Religion is the way to give up and is needed only for the weak person." Then I should try to explain the character of Sunyata with all my power by writing this book, and if I can make people recognize the necessity of living as trainers of the Bodhisattva Way, and recognize that it is the only way of correct human life, I should say there is no more thankful, enjoyable matter.

Buddhism is not denying that everything is changing but declaring it. But only form is changing, because it was born and will die. And empty form is not changing because it was not born and will not die. If something was born, it must die. If your baby was born, sooner or later he will die. The parents of human children should teach them this matter of fact at first. The enjoyable ceremony for having the birthday each year should be also the ceremony of death. Whatever the ceremony, it should always be concerned with our life and our death. Otherwise ceremony will become the low, slight, ghostly phenomenon. Ceremony should be the beautiful, meaningful, profound acts of human beings. It should be the dynamic harmony of contrasting human life. Anyway human children should know at the earliest possible age that they will die. Then a child will not have the silly desire to seek only such mortal and relative matters as the five objects of the five organs.

For instance, there is the person who loves to collect a lot of money. He may count his money after everyone goes to bed in the night. The merchant of darkness, thief, will visit him. Then this person must hide the money by his respectable life. In some case he will be killed by the thief. Even if such a terrible thing does not happen, generally the one who loves money must worry while sacrificing his own respectable life, keeping a hundred dogs and contriving an alarm wire to the police station at all windows of his house. But finally he trusts no one, not even the police. His life is not for him but only for his money. Generally the thief is the worker to collect the money. Then when he enters into our house we should give money to him. If he gets money it is likely he will not kill you.

A Japanese priest, Ryokan (died 1831), was very poor. While he was going out from his humble cottage a thief entered. On returning home he found nothing left, but there was a shining moon through the window. He said to himself, "Sorrowful thief, he forgot to steal that moon!"

This moon is not only the name of a planet which is far distant from our life. This moon is our mind which is Sunyata, not form.

One day a Zen priest, Ikkyu (died 1481), was surrounded by a group of bandits in the deep mountain. Ikkyu said, "I have no money, but I have the real treasure which is the Buddha Law." The leader of the bandits demanded, "Where is the Buddha Law?" "It is in my three inches chest," replied Ikkyu. The head bandit held a sharp knife and drew near. "Let me see!" Ikkyu was very calm and brilliantly made a poem:

> The cherry blossoms each year
> bloom on Yoshino Mountain
> Try to see where is the flower
> by cutting the trees.

In the story this bandit became a disciple of Ikkyu. The bandit might have killed Ikkyu indeed. Even if he had done so, still the moon, or the flower, or Sunyata will not die. Only our form will die or change.

Zenji Mugaku Sogen (1226–1286) is the founder of Enkaku-ji at Kamakura in Japan. He was Chinese, of the Southern Sung Dynasty. At that time the power of Yuan was rising all over China. And while Zenji Sogen was training at Mount Ganto the army of Yuan attacked this mountain also. Several soldiers grasped the Zenji to cut him with a broad-sword. But he was not disturbed at all, did not move even his eyebrows under the sword brandished over his head, and made a poem:

In this wide world there is not a place even to stand a stick,
How enjoyable a thing, human being is empty,
And Dharma is also empty.
This respectable three foot sword of great Yuan,
Cuts as a lightning flash cuts the spring air.

Zenji Mugaku Sogen was looking at the Sunyata which can not be born and not be ruined in the forms. His surprisingly penetrating understanding of Sunyata made the soldiers feel great respect, and they did not kill him. But even if he had been killed, nevertheless Sunyata will not die.

After we teach our children that we will die, we should teach them that the Sunyata which is every man's life, Buddha-nature, will not die. Only form will change as the character of the empty form which is life.

Teacher Shoin Yoshida was the enlightened leader of the movement to destroy old Japanese feudalism and to bring in the new democratic Meiji Era. Most great reformers of the Meiji Era were studying from him. But he was caught by the old government of Tokugawa and was killed at age thirty. He knew also his body will die but his Sunyata will not die, and he left a poem:

> Even though my body is ruined
> in the field of Musashi,[1]
> My spirit of Yamato[2]
> will continue to live.

He was always saying to his disciples, "If we don't enlighten about the problem of death-life, we cannot do any great thing."

Our body was born, if we think of fertilization as the beginning of life. Or our body will die, if we think of the stopping of the heart or the brain as death. It is just as if we were to say this world began in the year 5,000 B.C., which was momentarily settled as the beginning for the convenience of our poor brain. But fertilization is a step of life, it is not a beginning at all. Fertilization is the cause of a babyhood and at once the effect of the parents' lives. That being so, we can say the marriage of parents is the beginning of life also. The same thing can be said of our grandparents. And finally we can say the beginning of the universe is the beginning of life. We were born with the universe, not twenty or forty or eighty years ago. Of course still we are counting our form, body, as our age, but it is only to be seen with our poor physical instruments. Our Sunyata, life itself, however, was born with the universe and will die with the universe. But there is no beginning of the universe and also no end of the universe. Therefore we should say we, Sunyata, will not be born and also not be ruined. Our fingernails will die as we can easily see, but who will cry about that? We rather enjoy our nails dying. About our body we can say the same thing. The changing of our body is rather a thankful enjoyable thing. But fortunately our life itself will not die. Among Zen koans there is the following one:

> In the dark night, hearing the sound
> Of a crow which does not cry
> Makes me long to see my parents
> Who are not yet born.

This koan was made by Zenji Hakuin. The Zen trainer should be able to make a stanza in response for this stanza. If you can understand "not be born," naturally you can understand "not be ruined."

Living while awakening for eternal life makes the only real enjoyable mortal life. As to this point you may ask me, how should we live for the mortal if we know the eternal? This is a very contradictory, nonsensical question, because if you know the eternal you will know enough how you should live. But anyway I will answer, live with your best each moment.[3] If you finish eating breakfast, wash your dishes. When you want to go to the toilet, go sincerely. Even a small matter, do with all your will. If your child or parents die, cry for them. We are on the cross of eternity, the world of not-be-born and not-be-ruined. Live on the cross as your original nature, not by any other's opinion, discipline, philosophy. So, again, what is your original nature?

In the sentences of the Sutra occurring at the beginning of this lecture there are six "not's." Even if there were a hundred, you can understand in the same way as not-be-born and not-be-ruined. The important thing is really to train with all of your life.

VIII Active Understanding of Mu

> Therefore in emptiness there is not form, sensation, thought, volition, and consciousness; and not eyes, nose, tongue, body, and mind; and not matter, sound, smell, taste, touch, and laws; and not the world of eyes, . . . until the world of consciousness.

> *Ze ko ku chu mu shiki, mu ju so gyo shiki, mu gen ni bi zets shin ni, mu shiki sho ko mi soku ho, mu gen kai nai shi mu i shiki kai,*

Here Sakyamuni Buddha explained emptiness in more detail for the people who cannot understand ten by hearing one. Zen Master Itsugai scolded me always saying, "Understand ten by hearing one." Teaching too much to students makes less value of teacher. Even in a normal family if the husband asks his wife, "Please bring cigarettes," the wife should bring at least an ashtray and a matchbox. If the wife asks her husband to wash a spoon, he should wash all the bowls or forks in the sink. In the first case of the *Hekigan-roku* are written sayings with the following meanings: If you see smoke over the mountain, you can understand there is a fire. Still you should understand whether that smoke is from a forest fire or from a charcoal kiln or from a cooking oven. If you see two horns over a fence, you should understand whether it is a cow, goat, or sheep. If you see the corner of a square box you should know the other corners are there without seeing them. If you are a merchant you should be able to measure the weight or know the value of goods just by seeing them. A hotel boy will criticize the guests by seeing only their shoes, which is almost too hateful. Nevertheless, we should understand more than words. If we meditate, this kind of power will progress.

Seeing dull people, however, is very sorrowful. In fact, since childhood I have not been so sharp. So I feel unspeakable thanks to the person who tries to explain to me by all means, who is like Sakyamuni Buddha. Indeed the endurance to teach or to study is Buddha mind.

Here Sakyamuni Buddha is saying that in the emptiness, if you see form as emptiness, there are no Five Skandhas, six organs, six objects of six organs, and all worlds. World means the limited category of classification (*dhātu* in Sanskrit). The six organs are six worlds. And the six objects are another six worlds. Both of these six worlds will meet each other: for the eyes, matter, and for the nose, smell, etc. When they meet each other, another six worlds will arise, namely the world of seeing, the world of hearing, and so on. Then, totally, eighteen worlds will be counted from the world of eyes . . . until the world of consciousness. The world of consciousness will arise between the laws (objects which will be caught by consciousness) and consciousness. Then eighteen worlds means all worlds, and all of them are empty. This is because each of them is arising as the harmony of momentary mutual helping, and Cause and Effect, and has no ultimate substance, as I showed before.

Sakyamuni Buddha made various people enlighten with the kindly, suitable way for each person. One time there was a mother who lost her child and was crazy with desperation and grief. Finally she thought to visit Buddha for consulting about her suffering, and asked with tears, "I am crying because I lost my child who was my only son. Please will you make him come alive with your great power?" She was very sincere and Buddha felt the same sorrow with her and said, "It is really a miserable situation. Then return to your village one time and please bring a branch from the garden tree of a house in which no person ever died. If you do so, I may satisfy your hope." The mother enjoyed very much and ran to her village. She dashed into her neighbor's house and exclaimed, "Had you any funeral? I think you had not. Now I must get a branch." And she explained why. "What are you saying? Just this spring we lost our daughter," replied the neighbor. "Oh, excuse me." And the mother

Active Understanding of Mu

went to the next neighbor hurriedly and asked the same thing. This neighbor replied, "I lost my husband last year. I have my experience of losing my child also, which is very sorrowful. But losing my husband is miserably worse. Whenever I remember the time my husband was living with me, it makes me cry." And she cried. The mother visited the next and the next, and all houses of her village. But after all she could not find any house in which a person had not once died. She was surprised by the fact and fortunately by this understood Buddha's mind. "He wanted to teach me that if something was born certainly it will die, which is the Law. I should not stay in the sorrow so much. By knowing clearly this Law I should live strongly." And she apologized and thanked Buddha.

I heard from my grandmother that her husband never angered when she destroyed a dish or treasured furniture by accident. He would say, "All forms will ruin sooner or later." Grandmother also said to me, "He was a very sincere person. He worked all day for the laymen or garden but in the night he studied the sutras and many nights he stayed awake very late. When I said to him, 'Please rest, you can study tomorrow also,' his reply was often the same, 'There is no tomorrow.'"

In Japan there was a poor priest who loved to gamble. Whenever he got a little money he gambled. He always lost, and all furniture and dress went away. And he angered about his competitors and comforted himself finally, saying, "Heh! they also are the ones who must die." This poor priest knew half of the truth at least.

There is the following poem by Shelley called "Lines":

> When the lamp is shattered,
>   The light in the dust lies dead;
> When the cloud is scattered,
>   The rainbow's glory is shed;
> When the lute is broken,
>   Sweet tones are remembered not;
> When the lips have spoken,
>   Loved accents are soon forgot.

This poem with its feminine ending lines also is telling half the truth of the Hannya Sutra. From here the masculine ending poem should appear. Everything is changing, dying, ruining, returning into emptiness. Therefore we should think that harmony, mutually helping, is the most important thing. We cannot live alone. We should live in the air of thankfulness for everything. Among country people sometimes we can find such a person who is thankful for everything.

There was an old woman who had two sons who were merchants in the city. The elder brother was selling umbrellas and the younger brother was selling shoes. When it was a rainy day, this old woman complained, saying, "Oh, bad weather, my younger son cannot sell his shoes," and when it was a sunny day, this old woman complained, saying, "Oh, bad weather, my older son cannot sell his umbrellas." Though we can understand her mind to worry about her sons, she is seeing only the bad side of the truth. A priest taught to her, "Please think about your older son who is selling umbrellas when it is a rainy day, and think about your younger son who is selling shoes when it is a sunny day. You can live enjoyably." Then from that time she could live without complaining, but with thankfulness all the time.

Lack of the thankful mind comes from seeing the truth with half blindness. If we fully open our eyes, we can live in friendship with anyone, anything. Friendship is the most beautiful flower on this land. One arrow is easily broken, but two are hard to break.

When I was pilgrimaging in Japan after training in the monastery, I went to Tsushima, a southern island from which we can see Korea on fine days. I was walking on a mountain path where there were prickly thorn bushes, and a branch caught the long sleeve of my black robe. Momentarily I tried to separate them by force. As soon as I did so, I noticed that by doing such an unfriendly conduct both my robe and the thorn would get hurt. Both are living beings and should have friendship.

Thinking about friendship I hurried on my way to a village. After a dark, thick, thorny path suddenly I came out onto a cliff of pine forest. I could hear the sound of waves. And far below I could see white waves spreading on the black rocks through green branches of pine trees. I felt the solitary traveler cannot share with another this kind of wonderful feeling, seeing such a sight, though when I was in a hard situation I enjoyed that I was the only one receiving such things without needlessly giving them to others.

Gradually waves bagan to color by the sunset. My destination of that day was very near, the distance from eyes to nose, and I lay down to rest a little on the pine needles. But maybe I was very tired for I fell into a deep sleep, and it was when I felt a cool touch on my arm that I half waked. As soon as I saw with slightly opened eyes the black, long, crawling thing I was reminded of the caution which was spoken by a village hunter. This place was famous for its great number of poisonous snakes, vipers which can kill human beings within one hour if we don't get a shot to counter the poison. But even from the next village to the town would have taken five hours by car, if someone had such a thing. Mainly they were still using horses.

Without moving my body I carefully observed the creature on my right arm. The shape of its head was triangular, which was the exact feature described by the village hunter. And on its skin I saw the design was like a chain of coins. It was rather fat and short, and felt to me very tough and dynamically active, all of which made me certain this was a viper. I could not move because I knew it could jump to bite quickly. Then shutting my eyes, I had deep breaths a few times. That time I remembered the friendship with a thorn on the path. And I thought, "If this boy or girl snake likes to play with me, why shouldn't I play? I am not such a busy person." I opened my palm slowly. Thereupon that poisonous snake crawled into my palm from my arm and rested its neck between my thumb and forefinger. At that moment as I grasped it tightly, it coiled around my hand and stuck out its double tongue. Though it was sorrowful for the snake, I needed to live for me also. So I thrust up my hand with the snake and swung vigorously. When the poisonous snake uncoiled from my arm and became like a rope, I threw it over the ocean of sunset, chanting the Hannya-shin-gyo.

For the training to have thankfulness and find friendship, getting illness is a very good occasion. Since old times it has been said, "The person who does not know poorness, illness and disappointed love, does not know religion." As for that, though there is the person who knows all these three, still he may not know religion. Because he does not know them more than physically, which is as phenomena, not as the Law. In any case, illness makes people wise.

At first, we should know we cannot get illness even when we want it, and we cannot avoid illness even when we don't want it. Illness is also a harmony of Cause and Effect and mutual relations. Therefore we are not free to get or avoid it. Then, second, we should know that if we get illness it came to our life with deep meanings, not by so-called chance or misfortune. This visitor to our life is very respectable and a very friendly one for us. Try to ask him, "From where, how did you come here, why?" He cannot answer these questions for you so easily. Indeed even if you ask yourself why you got such illness, can you answer so smartly? Do not say, please, such a thing as you ate a lot of popcorn yesterday at the movie theater. Even if you did, in some case you would not have gotten illness. And still you should ask why you ate it. Finally you should say, somehow you got illness by Cause and Effect and the mutual relations since the beginning of the universe.

If we understand this matter of fact, the third thing we must know is that we should welcome the illness and should be thankful and have friendship for it. You should take care about your illness as if it were your child or your great guest. You should not deny or chase out your good visitor. Meanwhile you should spend your time with it, nurse it very well, and play with it. Usually the guest who is served such good food with polite manners will get tired of staying in another man's house and will go out sooner or later. Seeing far into this point, Hippocrates, who has been called the father of medical science, said illness will mend naturally, the doctor will only help it. By understanding illness in this way, shouldn't we enjoy having illness also?

You may say, "But by illness if we die, what should we do?" I will say, about death-life, we ought to solve it by understanding this Hannya Sutra. But meanwhile I will say about the matter of illness, we will die one time anyway. If we get illness a hundred times in our

Active Understanding of Mu

life, we can mend ninety-nine times, but only one time we cannot mend by even the greatest doctor. No one can stop the physical death even if one can make an Empire State Building by the legs of mosquitoes.

By the way if I dare say for the person who says on his sickbed, "I want to die, please let me die," human nature, and not only we ourselves but all creatures want to live, and we should live by any means until nature lets us die. At first we should realize our life is not our own. It is not our freedom to die or to hurt as we like, regardless of whether it is for others or for our own life. If our body is ours, why should we get illness? There is no excuse for killing life unless we make more alive by doing so, which means we can kill only our ego.

A patient may say, "Dying is better, it is too much suffering to live with illness." Such a person should understand my above talking and know that he should not die for only his relief, as well as that he should not live for only his enjoyment. Another patient may say, "Dying is better, living makes others suffer for my sake." Thinking of another person is very respectable. But if one is really to think of others, please think one more step: can't I make others happy by my situation? Certainly if we have mind, while we are living we can make others happy. Even in the sickbed one can show the good example as a patient. If you are in the hospital, you can smile to the nurse or doctor. Isn't this making others happy? If there is a patient who knows enjoying the illness and who thanks all, and who smiles in the hospital, many people can get good influence. By any means the hospital is not only for the patients but also for the nurses, doctors, and all those who work there. A smile is necessary more than a hundred flowers. A human smile has the great power which can change all the air of a hospital, and of course of the family. Then nurse and doctor feel the value of living for the patient. We should know the doctor of nurses and doctors is the patient.

So knowing thankfulness for illness and enjoying the friendship with illness means to remember the people who take care of us and our illness directly or indirectly. Even one medicine will be served to us through thousands of lives of human beings, animals, plants and all other beings; even a single pillow case was presented to us by innumerable lives.

On these matters, even if we don't get illness we should have the same recognition. But as in the popular saying, "The healthy person does not know the worth of health," we will forget, or we should live sincerely almost forgetting such a thing. Then by the good occasion of illness we should have gratitude to the world of lives. And we should determine to live for others, not only for ourselves.

I have spoken very quickly about the life of enjoyment, thankfulness and friendship, with a few examples which are only metaphors from our daily life. Please don't stick particularly to the metaphors but please notice the hidden meanings.

I was talking about the sutra's 'not, not, not . . . .' Zenji Rinzai understood this part of the sutra very actively, not only by the passive way of understanding emptiness. And he said in his *Rinzai-roku* (*The Records of Rinzai's Sayings*):[1]

"Whoever the trainers be, if they don't make the karma by committing the five heaviest sins, they cannot be freed perfectly."

In common Buddhism it was said that committing the five heaviest sins makes the endless karma to fall into the *avīci* hell wherein the one who has sinned is punished in boiling copper surrounded by seven overlapping iron fortresses. But Zenji Rinzai is saying that we should commit them in order to get perfect freedom for understanding emptiness. For what he really meant let us have his soliloquy:

"Question: What is the karma by committing the five heaviest sins?

"Answer: Killing father, killing mother, injuring the body of Buddha, destroying the harmony of friendship and burning the sutras or images are the karma by committing the five heaviest sins."

Certainly such conducts are endless sins, not simple crimes. It is because they are destroying all greatness of human lives. In the following he explains in more detail.

"Question: What is the father?

"Answer: Ignorance is the father. You cannot get the origin of your arising or ruining mind even if you seek it. It is like an echo in the sky. 'Killing the father' means being free wherever you are.

We have very deep ignorance if we think 'this' or 'that', which is the act that detaches us from the truth. For instance, seeing a beautiful woman is not wrong, it is natural pure life. But if we begin to think a bit, "Where is her beauty—her eyes, nose, or . . .?", already we are very far from the true life. This thought which is ignorance creates all desires and klesas:[2] "Yes, her nose is beautiful. I would like to get her! I must get her!" Zenji Rinzai is saying that there is not any substance in our thought which arises or ruins in each moment. We are living in the delusion from morning until night. No-substance is like an echo in the sky. Even if we ring a bell, the sound of the bell will not make any path in the sky. Even if the sound finishes, it will not destroy anything in the sky. The sound of a bell is only a momentary harmony. It is just like making a cottage in the forest by gathering wood. While it is standing, there is a cottage; but if you take it apart, it will return to the original forest. Then if you understand this very well, you will be free from the ignorance, which means you killed the father.

In the same way Zenji Rinzai continued:

"Question: What is the mother?

"Answer: Blind love is the mother. Your mind will enter into the world of desire but even if you seek the substance of the blind love you will see only that everything is empty. Understanding in this way and being freed from attachment will be called 'killing the mother.' "

He is saying don't have illusions or delusions, enlighten. But even if you get enlightenment you should not be caught by it and live in very cruel self satisfaction. For such kind of persons he says next:

> "Question: What is the meaning of injuring the body of Buddha?
> "Answer: You will enter into the purity itself and not have any delusive mind; you will live as a body in any circumstances."

This does not mean to stay with enlightenment in the pure mountain. We should throw even the mind to think we got enlightenment. And in each situation we should not have any egoistic, dualistic thought. If you are a servant, you will do your best as a servant, forgetting your ego. If you are a worker in a company you will not think of your own matter but will work your best for the company.

In America there are too few people who are devoted to their work. Too many people think very much about their own matter. Teachers of schools have strikes. For what? To get more money! Are they really teachers? If they don't like to teach with given money, they mustn't become teachers. Teaching is a human, natural instinct to want to love others, to want to give something which we have to those who don't have. Where is there the person who will request money because he loves a girl? This can be said for any kind of worker. Anyway, we should have the revolution of the world so that people will not work for the money but only as their native wish to work. About this pure work of human beings if we see from the outside, it will become the helping of all sentient beings, as was said in the following sentences of Zenji Rinzai:

> "Question: What is the meaning of destroying the harmony of the friendship?
> "Answer: If you are through understanding that all klesas and desires are unsubstantial things, it will be called 'destroying the harmony of the friendship.'"

Without this understanding, in fact, we cannot live for others. And still we can progress further.

"Question: What is the meaning of burning the sutras or images?

"Answer: If you completely know that Cause and Effect is empty but it is the absolute, that our mind is empty but it is the absolute, and that the Dharma is also empty but it is the absolute as itself, and if you have no doubt, even a moment, you will be free from everything and will not be disturbed by anything, which means 'burning the sutras or images.' "

Well, Zenji Rinzai is really kind to us. All of these are true understanding of the emptiness, not only by our brain but by the body in practical life. Without this religious experience, the real humanity will not be presented on this earth.

IX Where Humanity Arises

There is not ignorance, and not the end of ignorance, . . . until not old age and death, and not the end of old age and death; there is not suffering, accumulation, annihilation, and the way; there is not wisdom, and not attainment because there is not that which can be attained.

mu mu myo, yaku mu mu myo jin, nai shi mu ro shi, yaku mu ro shi jin, mu ku shu metsu do, mu chi yaku mu toku, i mu sho toku ko.

Here in the Sutra the series of Twelve Steps of Cause and Effect, from ignorance to old age and death, were made empty by Prajna. If we are enlightened, there is no ignorance. Accordingly there is no end of ignorance, and this can be said for all Cause and Effect.

But without enlightenment if someone thinks there is no Cause and Effect, he will fall into hell quickly. Someone may say, in the form there is Cause and Effect but there is no Cause and Effect in the formless form. It is a good thought for a certain step towards understanding the truth, but it is not real truth at all. Originally we cannot divide to form and formless form. The Hannya Sutra already tells that form is formless form, and formless form is form. Therefore we should see that Cause and Effect itself is empty as suchness. Here, there is an interesting koan story from Case Two of *Mumon-kan*.

Whenever Zenji Hyakujo[1] preached, there was an old man among the monks hearing the Law. When the monks left this old man also left. But one day only this old man did not leave. Then Hyakujo asked him, "Who is standing in front of me?" "Ya, to say frankly, I am not a human being. I was a priest in this mountain in the age of Kasho Buddha, who was the Buddha of past time. At that time a trainer asked me whether the great enlightened trainer would fall into Cause and Effect or not. I replied, 'He will not fall into Cause and Effect.' That's why I fell into the fox life, being born and dying as a fox five hundred times. Now I beg you sincerely to answer one true living word to free me from the fox life." And he asked, "Will the great enlightened trainer fall into Cause and Effect or not?" Hyakujo answered, "No one can conceal the chain of Cause and Effect." As soon as the old man heard this saying he got enlightenment and after having worship said, "I already am freed from the fox life by you, and I will live behind this mountain. I dare to ask you, please have a funeral for me as a dead monk."

Hyakujo had the *Ino*[2] announce to all monks that in the afternoon the funeral for a dead monk would be performed. The monks wondered, saying such things as, "All of us are healthy. No one is entering into the Hall of Nirvana.[3] Why is there such an announcement?" After lunch, Hyakujo led the monks under a cliff behind the mountain. And it was seen that they picked up a dead fox with a stick and performed the cremation.

In the evening Hyakujo sat on the high lecture seat and spoke of the above episode to the monks. Then a disciple, Obaku, asked him, "The old man answered the one word incorrectly and fell into the fox life five hundred times, you said. But if each time he had not answered incorrectly, what would he have become?" Hyakujo said, "Come close to me. I will tell you." Obaku went up and gave him a slap. Hyakujo laughed, clapping his hands and said, "I was thinking only I am a red-bearded Bodhidharma, but here there was another one!"

About this koan, the important thing we should understand is whether the greatly enlightened (meaning whoever is a human being) fall into Cause and Effect or not? The Hannya Sutra is telling that there is no Cause and Effect if we practice the deep Prajna. If we practice the deep Prajna! Otherwise there is Cause and Effect and we fall into Cause and Effect.

But Hyakujo said, "No one can conceal the chain of Cause and Effect." "No one" means everyone whether great or not, without any exception. Then, finally what do all of these sayings mean for us? We should know there is freedom because there is no substance. But by the same reason, phenomena arise, which is unfreedom. So no-substance is the cause of freedom and unfreedom. We are not free because we are free, or we are free because we are not free. If you understand this strange, wonderful, mystical world you are the real human being among beings, who is not beast, not God. When you understand this contradictory but harmonious contrast, the cross, you will like to live and die on the cross.

Then you can say, what is wrong with living as a fox? Mumon says in his comment on this koan:

> Not fall into Cause and Effect; by this why did the old man fall into the fox life? Not to be able to conceal Cause and Effect; by this why could the old man be freed from the fox life? If you have one eye on these points, you can see that the former Hyakujo, the old man, was enjoying to live in such a tasty fox life, being born and dying as a fox five hundred times.

What is the fox? The fox is the real human life, living as one's nature in the nature. What is the real meaning of the Sutra lines: "There is not ignorance, and not the end of ignorance, . . . until not old age and death, and not the end of old age and death"? It is to live as the fox. For an active, practical explanation about this fox life I should bring here another koan, from the *Katto-shu, Mingling Vines of Ivy and Wisteria: Koan Collection*.[4]

> Once upon a time there was an old woman who was serving the priest of a temple while twenty years passed. Always she let a young girl serve the food. One day she had the girl embrace the priest and ask him, "How will you feel in this case?" The priest replied, "It is like a dead tree standing on the cold rock which has no warmth during the three months of winter." His words were reported to the old woman and she said, "For twenty years I was serving this worldly person!" Then she burned the temple down.

The point which we should put our eyes on is the reply of the priest which tests our understanding of emptiness. If we really understand it, how should we live? What is the real humanity which goes beyond ignorance and enlightenment? Even if we make empty the Cause and Effect, it is only making worse karma. Why couldn't this priest be freed from emptiness? Generally while there are two opponents war will not end and the real freedom of peace will not appear. While we see the mountain and the ocean, already there is no freedom and no sameness. Because when we see them as parts of mountain-and-ocean, already we are making differences, the cause of fighting. Indeed, we cannot divide, we cannot draw any clear line between them; they are one.

As an example in more daily life, if we think 'wife' and 'husband' already there is cause enough for fighting. As human, natural harmony, we cannot divide them to two. Still, if we divide to wife and husband, already the unnatural insisting of each others' egos will appear. They are one. Though they will live as two sometimes, when they face their child they should always live as one. Therefore we cannot say 'wife' and 'husband,' but can say only 'wife of husband' and 'husband of wife.' Then there is no fighting between them. When we see the whole world as one, there is peace and sameness. Still in one there is enough wonderful peculiarity of each thing and there are harmonious contrasts, but not ego and contradictions. This priest was still clinging to the empty part, dividing this world to two, that of emptiness and that of being. Our free, real, enjoyable Bodhisattva life will come only when we live in the one, which was the tasty fox life.

Another point to see in this koan is about "she burned the temple down." What did she burn? Was she not so kindly a woman? From a carp she made a dragon, from a rooster she made a phoenix. Otherwise, how can we help ourselves and others? Helping sentient beings is like trying to bury a well by filling it with snow.

On the same matter as the above is the saying of a respectable old Zenji, Shoju (1641–1721), teacher of Zenji Hakuin:

> It is easy to endure intolerable suffering if you think that it lasts only a day. About enjoyment as well, if you think that it lasts only

one day you will not be addicted to it. About being obedient to one's parents also, if you think each single day, you should not have any quibbling. If you live each single day, and one day your endeavors are easy and you think it will last all your life, it becomes an exaggerated matter. Though you may think your whole life is long, in fact no one knows after that. If you think your death is the end, it is easy to perform your whole life. Your "most important thing" means "today," "the present mind." If you pay no attention to this there is no good tomorrow. Generally most people plan for the distant future, but they don't realize they are losing the now in this present moment.

Next, about "there is not suffering, accumulation, annihilation, and the way." These four are essential teachings of Buddhism for the practical life. Then we call these the Four Truths. To people who could not understand by their physical experience, without relying on analytical thinking, Sakyamuni Budda explained these Four Truths logically: what human life is, why it is so, then what we should do for it, and how. What human life is is suffering, about which I have already talked, the four basic sufferings of human life, described in the Lotus Flower Sutra simply:

> In the three worlds there is no safety, it is like a burning house, terrible, filled with various sufferings. Always there is the worrying over life, old age, illness, and death. Such fires of karma are burning furiously and never stop.

The "three worlds" are the deluded worlds which are arranged on three levels: (1.) the world of desires, in which a creature has two desires, carnal desires and sleeping desires, living in the six ways which are the ways of hell, hungry ghosts, beasts, fighters (*asuras,* in Sanskrit), men, and heaven; (2.) the world of form, in which a creature is separated from the two desiring lives; (3.) the world of formless form, in which the creature has gone beyond the form or material lives.

Anyway, the three worlds means all of our worlds, all life to which either spiritual or physical thought can refer. Life in the three worlds is suffering, which is the First Truth and the first step to the religious life. If we reflect on ourselves, no one can say he has no suffering. The Second Truth is that suffering is caused by "accumulation," which means ignorance or klesa is gathering the sufferings. Klesa can be inherited or acquired. Karl Marx tried to solve the simple suffering among human sufferings, economic or material suffering in the social world, but he did not try to solve the greater human sufferings, such as death, illness, and old age, which have almost no relation with social phenomena. Therefore the revolution of his successors was not worthy to be called so. Revolution means to be freed from klesa, which does not mean to cut off our desires but rather not to be attached to them. The important thought of Buddhism as to the cause of our suffering is that we don't say God or the first parents made the cause. Rather, we say we made it. If God made it, why should we try to solve our suffering with our power? Everything then depends on God. In the thought of God our respectable human possibility will be denied just as it is by nihilism. But if we made the cause of suffering, then we can solve our suffering with our human power. Then we should realize that all our sufferings were made by us and the cause for them is that we have original klesa or desire. In the *Sutra of Metaphor* there is a story which shows our situation:

> Once upon a time there was a traveler. When he was walking in a wide field, suddenly he met with a crazy elephant. He was surprised and tried to escape, but there was no place to hide because all around was the wide plain field. Fortunately there was an old well in the field. And in the well a vine of wisteria was hanging down. "Oh, thank heaven!" he exclaimed and he entered into the well down the vine. The horrible crazy elephant was looking into the well, showing its tusks. While the traveler was pausing after his successful escape, at the bottom of the well a large serpent was awaiting his falling with opened mouth. Shocked, the traveler looked all around and saw that there were four poisonous

snakes trying to bite him on all sides of the wall of the well. His life was depending only on the vine of wisteria. When he realized that, however, two rats, one white and the other black, were already gnawing the vine's root. It's all up! He could not feel he was alive. Just at that time it happened that from a comb of honey where bees were nesting on the root of the wisteria, a drop and another drop and five or so drops of honey dropped into his mouth. Those drops were so sweet, like the dew from heaven, that the traveler forgot the immediate danger and sought the drops of honey greedily.

Needless to explain, the traveler who is wandering on the wide field means us, human beings. The crazy elephant means the "wind of mortality" which is the flowing time. The well is the depth of our death-life, or the cliff of death-life. The large serpent in the bottom of the well means the shadow of death. The four poisonous snakes are the four elements which are constituting our bodies, and the vine of wisteria is our lives, the vine of life. The two rats, white and black, mean the daytime and the night. The five drops of honey mean the five desires, our human sensual desires, which are appearing when our five organs meet with their five objects.

Then what should we do? The Third Truth, "annihilation," will come in here. It means to get Nirvana, to blow out the fire of desires. For the question of how, the Fourth Truth, "the Way," will come. It means to practice the Eight Correct Ways which are: (1.) Correct Seeing (of the Four Truths), (2.) Correct Thinking (on the Four Truths), (3.) Correct Talking, (4.) Correct Living, (5.) Correct Following (of the Law), (6.) Correct Assiduity, (7.) Correct Memorizing (for the correct Way), (8.) Correct Meditation.

These are the same as the Six Paramitas.

About correct seeing, I should explain a little more. Though I say 'see', there are many different meanings such as 'look', 'gaze', 'watch', 'gape', 'glare', 'peek', 'peer', 'behold', 'espy', 'view', and so on. I want to mean all of these, but also none of them are the exact expression for me. A historically great swordsman, Musashi Miyamoto, known also as the artist Niten, wrote about sight in his book *Go-rin-sho* (*The*

Book of Five Wheels):[5] "It is an important matter for swordsmanship that having two eyes one of them is to see so that we see the far place as the near place and the other is to look so that we look at the near place as the far place. Seeing eyes should be strong and looking eyes should be weak. It is an important matter for swordsmanship that while knowing the enemy's sword we not see the sword of the enemy at all. And seeing to both sides without moving the eyeballs is also an important matter. You cannot discriminate such matters when you are busy or in the midst of sudden necessity. Then memorize these sayings and study these points about sight and no-moving eyes very well in your daily life."

By only reading these sayings, you can imagine the swordsman Musashi. But he was not a simple swordsman. In the same book, in "The Chapter of Emptiness" he writes, "Don't be lazy, but polish in the morning and evening your two minds, which are the conscious and unconscious minds, and sharpen your two eyes, which are the seeing and looking eyes. And when you clear up all your clouds of delusion, it can be called the real emptiness."

Then I hope you will understand what is meant by "Correct Seeing." It is not only seeing the Four Truths objectively, but being in the objects. This correct seeing is one of the most important practices of religion because it is the eyes for walking. And another important thing is Correct Assiduity, which is the feet for walking.

Before a disciple, Purnama, went to a country of pagans to preach, he greeted the Teacher. The Teacher, Sakyamuni Buddha, asked him, "My Purnama, the people of the country are brutal and do not have enough culture. Therefore they may abuse, insult and shame you. Are you aware of these things?" "My Buddha, I will have gratitude, thinking they are sensible enough to abstain from beating me with stone or tile even though they abuse, insult, and shame me." "My Purnama, the people of the country are having strong brutality. And they may beat you with stone or tile. What will you do in such a case?" "My Buddha, I will have gratitude thinking they have mercy not to kill me with sword even though they beat me with stone or tile." "My Purnama, if they are indeed really brutal and if they hurt or kill you with sword, what will you do?" "My Buddha, in such a time I will think that they have real mercy to free me from such a body which is a receptacle of klesa and evil karma, and I will have gratitude to them." Finally Buddha said, "My Purnama, how good, how good you are, preach the Way to all of the country of pagans with your tolerant assiduity." And Buddha sent him to the foreign country to build the enlightened world.

If we continue our assiduity, there is nothing we cannot do if it is a good thing for us. Even a tiny stream can make round the rocks. Even a tiny fire if it continues can boil the water in the kettle.

Well, I explained the Four Truths, suffering, accumulation, annihilation, and the Way. The Hannya Sutra also tells us that there are not these Four Truths, if we make clear about our original nature. Otherwise, practice the Four Truths, which can be called giving up trying to solve our sufferings. At least give up trying to solve the sufferings of human life. Even by such giving up you can at least get your own satisfaction. A Bodhisattva, however, should make clear the Four Truths by practicing, by knowing what our original nature is. Then you will understand there are not these Four Truths also.

Next is on "there is not wisdom, and not attainment because there is not that which can be attained." This means while there are not the Four Truths, naturally there is not to-be-blinded and not to-be-enlightened by those truths. Therefore there is no wisdom and also not anything to be attained, and there is not attainment also. Wisdom is like medicine which is not necessary after the patient mends his illness. Furthermore, if he still uses medicine, it turns to poison for him.

According to Zen tradition, when Bodhidharma came to China he was asked by the Emperor Bu, "I built many temples, edited many sutras and helped many monks since I ascended the throne. What kinds of merit are there for me?" "There is not any merit," was the reply of Bodhidharma. If you have been hearing my talking all along, you will understand that his answer was not merely at the level

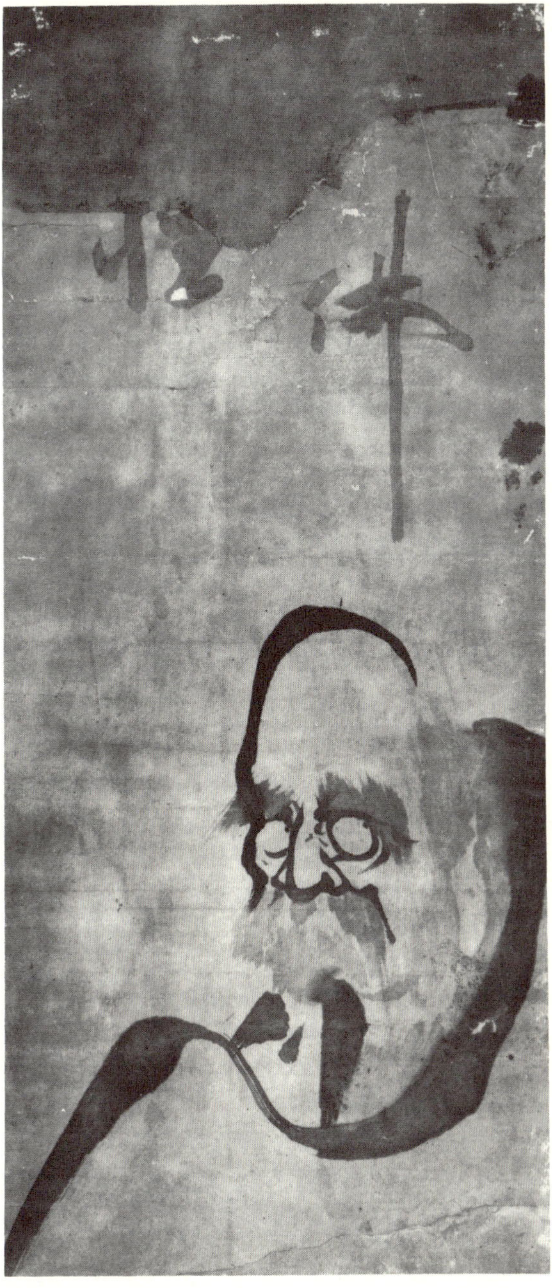

of social morality, not like such sayings as 'the morality which was performed for the morality,' or 'the great person who became so while thinking to become a great person is not really a great person.' The saying of Christ, "But when thou doest alms, let not thy left hand know what thy right hand doeth" (Matthew 6:13) also should not be understood as a new morality against the old morality. If you understand it as only a morality, you are already one of the Pharisees. As social morality you should rather let your left hand know what your right hand does. Otherwise you cannot avoid being called a stoic or ghost. If you like to let know, let know as you like. Some day you will be awakened to "there is not that which can be attained." Saint Paul, also, said, "We reckon therefore that a man is justified by faith apart from the works of the law" (Romans 3:28).

Otherwise how can you understand the following dialogue? The Emperor asked, "What is the essence of Buddhist teachings?" Bodhidharma answered, "It is empty, there is not even a sacred thing." He said it is not anything, like a fine autumn sky without even a cloud. If we say sacred, already it is a relative thing which is not the essence. How great Bodhidharma is! Don't you want to have such mind? The Emperor could not understand the answer of Bodhidharma, unfortunately. Then finally he asked Bodhidharma on a very normal social level, "Who are you?" meaning, 'I cannot understand anything of your sayings. I was doing good matters and seeking the sacred matters, but you denied such things. That means you also are not a great Patriarch at all. But I was hearing you are great. Indeed who are you?' Bodhidharma replied, "I don't know." There is no more honest person than Bodhidharma. He was answering really kindly for the Emperor, but showing directly truth itself. Though modern people introduce themselves, really are they knowing who they are? At least Bodhidharma knew he does not know. We call such a person the Avalokitesvara, awakened one, or Buddha.

To Zenji Joshu a monk asked, "What should I do while I am not bringing to you even a thing?" Joshu answered, "Throw it away!" If we get the wisdom we should throw it. The real training is really a difficult thing. We should train all our life without stopping even a day. To where should we throw it? Live as a Bodhisattva. Wisdom is love with sorrow. Love is wisdom. Then one more time I will ask what is the meaning of "there is not that which can be attained"? This is the essence of Buddhism, of life itself.

In Japan I have often heard Buddhist priests say "be like it," meaning if you are a woman "live like a woman," if you are a mother "live like a mother," if you are a student "live like a student," and so on. Certainly if we live in that way, the beautiful world will appear, it seems so. But in my opinion, we should know before "like it." Otherwise we are still the slave of an idea, or an idol, or all forms. We should "be as it." "Be as it" means "there is not that which can be attained" because there is not any more subject and object while we are in the subject and the object. We should know there is not our ideal thing in this world. But there are perfect things. Our un-ideal situation or un-ideal enlightenment is the perfect situation and the perfect enlightenment. Because perfectness is when we see our beings, but the ideal is not when we see our beings. Don't seek the ideal but seek the perfectness! Even a painting, if it was drawn by an artist to show the ideal, don't you feel somehow it has no relation with your practical life? Art should be the expression of perfectness which is un-ideal. We should not be as an ideal person but should be a perfect person, and fortunately we are so. The only problem is that most people don't see this fact. Perfectness means imperfectness, which means being with thousands of contrasted beings as knowing so. "I love the fool" was the saying of the English essayist Charles Lamb. If I dare to correct in my way, "I love the fool who knows he is the fool."

> I ate a lot of poison grass,
> And saw many falling stars
> On the cliff in front of my cave,
> But I did not die, did not hate.
> Let me go to the village to turn on the light.

X Freedom, The Life of No Attainment

Bodhisattva has no obstacles in his mind, because he is living in the Prajna-paramita, and he has no fears because there are no obstacles; he has gone far beyond delusions and illusions, and perfected Nirvana.

Bo dai sats ta, e han nya ha ra mi ta ko, shin mu ke ge, mu ke ge ko, mu u ku fu, on ri its sai ten do mu so, ku gyo ne han.

When I was a child, my mother took me on a bus trip and she said to me, pointing to the turning color of the maple forest with the white mist of an autumn rain behind the fresh green bamboo groves, "All those mountain sights are mine! How rich I am!" "Why are all of those yours?" I wondered. "Because they will enter into my eyes freely and disappear freely," she replied. At the time I thought I understood but later I lost my sense and these days again I think her sayings had great meaning. She does not carry anything in her mind. Therefore all things can enter and go out freely without any obstacles.

All people, when they go abroad to study from another country, should go with an empty mind like a piece of white paper. Otherwise they will get only the delusive cultures which were built on the rusty sands of their own culture. They will impose a heavily prejudiced view on other countries and an incoherent view on their own country, like grafting a tree onto bamboo.

Having the mind of "no attainment" makes us really free persons.

Let me show a pure dew drop. If you put it on a green camelia leaf it turns green, but if you put it on a red camelia petal it turns red. It can become a square form, triangular, round, etc. Furthermore, it can change to vapor, ice, rain, steam. But still it is H_2O, whenever. How free this creature is! Because it has the mind of "no attainment." It is in our bodies also.

Most people cannot welcome their guests into their homes because they feel a kind of obstacle in their mind. They can welcome guests only when they have prepared their homes by cleaning very well. That means while we have dust within us, we cannot welcome other people. Therefore we should clean ourselves all the time. That is the only way to have no obstacle in our minds. But if we realize our own original nature we cannot attain anything. Naturally there is no obstacle for us. If there is no obstacle, even without our trying all kinds of guests are coming and going freely. Even if you don't try to hear the sound of airplanes while you are reading, why will the sound enter into your ears?

In Zen paintings there is often a picture of Priest Hotei with a happy smiling face and large stomach, carrying a huge bag on his back. In Japan he is considered one of the seven gods of good fortune. Though the color of dress is different, I think he is the same as Santa Claus in Western tradition, each gives happiness to us. Then we should think, what are they carrying in their bags? You may think a lot of cakes, jewels, money, but they don't have such things. Their bags are, in fact, empty. Smiling, they will give to us the emptiness, and smiling they will take into their large stomachs all our sufferings. Otherwise they are unworthy of being called ambassadors of God.

Here there is a koan from *Mumon-kan*, Case Ten:

> A great trainer, Seizei, asked to Priest Sozan, "I am alone and poor, my teacher, please help me." Sozan addressed him, "My respectable trainer!" "Yes," Seizei replied. Then Sozan said, "Though you have drunk three full cups of the best alcohol produced in Seigen, still you are saying you don't even wet your lips."

Seizei was a great trainer who already was going beyond the social poorness or aloneness. Furthermore, even though he was physically so, he would not ask to another about matters which were his responsibility, saying "Please help." Modern people are not only begging help from such places as the government, but they are also shamelessly forcing the government to help them, without willingly paying taxes and without reflecting on their way of living. And weak governors, who are seeking useless admiration as if they were movie actors, are trying to help the people only physically, not by cultivating their mind for their real freedom. The parents of frogs are frogs and the children of frogs are also frogs. If we are poor and alone in the social world, at first we should try to understand why we are so and really are we so? Do not say, because of the government, which as you know has no power over our freedom.

Then what did Seizei mean in his saying, "I am alone and poor"? "Alone" means "one" which is not divided to two or more by any means. For instance, if you make the subject and object, already you are not alone. If you settle God outside of you, already such God will not help you at all. Because then there are two worlds. One is the world of God and the other is your world. Even if you try to lay a bridge between yourself and God, still there are two worlds which were divided, imperfect as half of the whole world. While we don't see the world as a whole, as one, our work to build the bridge will be useless, an empty waste. Furthermore, you would fight finally with God. Because, if there are contrasting oppositions, as their character they will fight if we don't see them as one. But if we see them as one they will have friendship spontaneously.

Anyway, Seizei was the universe itself which is alone. And accordingly he had not any contradictory views such as enlightened world and klesa world, or beautiful and dirty. Naturally he had not any dualistic philosophy, morality, or any such false riches. He was poor. Therefore his asking to Priest Sozan was not so simple a question or begging, but was to test the priest. Priest Sozan could see Seizei's intention.

Priest Sozan was not pulled into the secondary discussion of ideas. He presented the nature of the universe itself by addressing Seizei, who was nature itself, and Seizei replied, "Yes." Both of them are great, and kindly trying to show us the world of "no attainment" by their true acting. And Priest Sozan commented, "Though you have drunk three full cups of the best alcohol produced in Seigen, still you are saying you don't even wet your lips." In China, "three" often means "all" or "many." "You" does not specify Seizei but means all human beings, us. We human beings all are rich enough but still we are seeking more. We are not enjoying the things which we have but only seeking the things which we don't or can't have. Then Mumon asked to us, "What does it mean that the respectable trainer drank his fill of alcohol?"

Even if you understand these matters, it is not enough if you really cannot live the life of "no attainment."

In old times there was a great Chinese scholar, Tokusan (782–865), who was not pleased with Zen teachings, such as "This mind itself is the Buddha," or "We are originally Buddha." Then for the purpose of refuting Zennists he traveled through all prefectures until he came to Rei.

There was a trea restaurant where an old woman was selling rice cakes. "Hey, grandma, please sell the rice cakes, two or three," Tokusan said to her.

But this old woman asked him, "What will you do with these cakes?"

"I will eat them to let my mind work."

"Ha-han, I see. Well if you can answer for my question I will offer them to you free. But if you cannot answer enough for me I will not sell them. At first, what are you carrying which is such a large burden on your back?"

"These are interpretations which I wrote about the Diamond Prajna Sutra. For what are you asking such a thing?"

"It's not another matter. I would like to ask about a part of the Sutra which I am not sure how to understand."

Tokusan said, "Ask me anything, if it concerns the Diamond Prajna Sutra!"

"Then let me ask. In the Sutra it was said, 'The mind of past time is not able to be gotten, the mind of present also is not able to be gotten, and the mind of future also is not able to be gotten.' Now answer me, to which mind will you feed the cakes and let it work?"

Tokusan could not reply even half a word.

The old woman said, "Please buy cakes in another shop. You cannot be free by only the interpretation."

But he was indeed a great scholar who at least had not strange pride, and asked her, "You are a disconcerning one, but how did you come to be so?"

The old woman said, "There is a great Zenji, Ryutan, nearby. You also visit to study, at least until you will not be shamed by an old woman."

Then Tokusan burned all his work of interpretation and trained under Ryutan. Later he became a redwood of the Zen forest, as well known as Rinzai.

Without real training we cannot testify the real freedom. We should practice the deep Prajna-paramita. The Sutra tells that Bodhisattva Avalokitesvara is living in the Prajna-paramita. Therefore there are no obstacles in his mind. In theory, Prajna is one of the Six Paramitas, but in fact six is one, one is six. Donation is the face, precepts the hand, perseverance another hand, assiduity the legs, Dhyana the body, and Prajna the mind. All are one body of human being. If there are no obstacles, there are no fears which come because we have delusions and illusions.

In an old folk story there was a monkey who discovered the beautiful moon on a pure lake surrounded by deep woods. While enjoying seeing the moon, he tried to seize it by hanging onto a branch with one hand and his tail, and reaching down with the other hand, but his hand did not reach the moon. Then he called his friends, four or five. And they hung by grasping hand in hand. But as soon as the first monkey put his hand into the water to get the moon, wave circles appeared and the moon escaped. They tried and tried repeatedly but finally they could not get the moon and they looked admiringly at it from the bank.

By hearing this story, a little bit clever person will laugh. But such a person is laughing at the monkey's hip without seeing his own hip. We human beings evolved from monkeys (at least about these matters) and are doing the same kind of things. It is a sorrowful fact.

When I was an elementary school boy, one Sunday morning I woke up and saw my mother who was working in her overalls in the garden. I complained to her, "What are you doing? Please change your dress quickly and make yourself up!" My mother was surprised by my sudden saying. "You promised to take me to town today! If you don't hurry we will miss the bus," I continued. My mother was perplexed a minute and then began to laugh, saying, "Oh, you, my child. You had a dream!" I angered, but gradually as if mist were going away from the mountain, my brain became clear and I noticed her promise was made in my dream. Suddenly I had a very strange feeling, I cannot say it was enjoyment or sorrow, maybe both. And I burst into tears. My mother was kind to me and promised to take me to town. Then I was a country boy who wanted to see the crowded town. But the real promise was also a dream.

> How thankful!
> The person who lives in the dream,
> The person who lives while awakening,
> Both are in the dream,
> The same way of human being.

I am not sure of the difference between the English words illusion and delusion. Maybe it is only a difference of degree. If delusion is the opposite idea of truth, then illusion can include the meaning of delusion and a wider sense. In that sense if I talk, delusions are counted as four since old times in Buddhism, those being eternity, enjoyment, substance, and purity. Eternity means thinking there is an eternal thing in this world, as in the belief in the immortality of the soul. There is the soul, therefore it will change. Enjoyment means thinking this world of human beings is an enjoyable thing. Enjoyment should be the other name of suffering. Substance means believing there is ego in each thing, or God in the universe as the supervisor or as the creator of the world. There is ego or God, but they have no substance. Therefore they are free beings. Purity means thinking that our human bodies are pure. There is purity, but not in our thinking. Therefore our bodies can become the Bodhi-tree and can train in the Bodhisattva Way.

All four of these are delusions. Now Bodhisattva Avalokitesvara went far beyond these delusions and illusions. He is not detached from the human world physically but he can live freely to help sentient beings. That is why it was said in the following sentences of the Lotus Flower Sutra:

> Bodhisattva Mujinni asked to Sakyamuni Buddha with full respect, "My Buddha, how does Bodhisattva Avalokitesvara visit this *Sahā*[1] World in which we should have patience for our klesas and sufferings? What is the power of his helping ways?" Buddha said to Bodhisattva Mujinni, "My wise one, if there are sentient beings in any country who are to be saved by the form of Buddha, Bodhisattva Avalokitesvara will present himself in the Buddha form and preach for them the Dharma. For the beings who are to be saved by the form of self-enlightenment by observing Cause and Effect, he will present himself in the self-enlightened form and preach for them the Dharma. For the beings who are to be saved by the form of attained-enlightenment by hearing the teaching, he will present himself in the attained-enlightenment form and preach for them the Dharma. For the beings who are to be saved by the form of God as the protector, he will present himself in the form of God and preach for them the Dharma. For the beings who are to be saved by the form of . . . ."

He can be in any form for saving suffering sentient beings. If you think God or the enlightened one are staying in the physical purity, you are insulting them. They are all the time acting to give the enjoyment to us and to take the suffering out from us in the world of forms.

Freedom, The Life of No Attainment 153

In old times Diogenes was looking with a lamp for something at a street corner of Athens in the daytime. His disciple who happened to pass asked him, "Teacher, what are you looking for? Did you lose something?"

Diogenes said, "I am looking for the man."

"The man? Many people are coming along, aren't they?"

This philosopher said cooly, "They are not men!"

Indeed there are not great men, if we seek a certain form which is our illusion. Diogenes, at least in this story, had not eyes to see the Bodhisattva Avalokitesvara. If we have eyes to see, we can see many men; if we don't have eyes, even if we look for a man with a lamp in the daytime, still we cannot find him. Even in a brothel there are such great women:

In my treasure box I have an Eleven Faces Avalokitesvara image which was transmitted to each of my family's ancestors. Originally this was given to an ancestor when she married from the wife of a lord. When my family faced the misery of poverty I almost determined to sell it, but while I was having the last worship for our separation somehow my mind opened and could be taught something. Finally I could not sell it, and brought it into this dirty room. It seems very impious treatment but I am depending on this Avalokitesvara and saying my greetings to many mistaken men at the morning parting as a real Japanese woman, whole-heartedly. I will send them off hoping they will not lose their way to live correctly again, hoping they will not enter into this kind of world deeply. Their ears would not hear the cautions from their parents or brothers, but they could hear my advice, a girl in the brothel. People say prostitutes are lowly beings but no one can say that so easily. Since old times there were many excellent people among the prostitutes, not only in Yoshiwara. Thinking that I was sold to this place by my father-in-law makes me sad, but I want to serve sincerely as the training of a Bodhisattva with this body, and I want to have worship for the happiness of my dead parents and my family and all people. You also please serve the people with Buddha mind. Our Sakyamuni Buddha taught us kindly. Especially his teaching about Avalokitesvara is thankful because according to his teaching, Avalokitesvara can save us, whatever our sufferings are, by changing its form to our form. Whatever the life is, it is not suffering at all. Happiness and unhappiness are depending on the bottom of one's mind. Let us train in the Bodhisattva Way hand in hand!

(This is a real story recorded in the book *The Enjoyment of Dharma Without Hands* by the nun, Reverend Junko Oishi.) [2]

Some people complain or worry about the waning of religion, in the Eastern world the ebb tide of Buddhism, and in the Western world the ebb tide of Christianity. But ebb tides are only carrying away the old shells, which is an enjoyable natural phenomenon. Sakyamuni Buddha lived for the people, Christ died for the people; that fact is never carried away by the ebb tide.

"And perfected Nirvana" means to live for other people and to let them live by themselves with the mind of "no attainment" of which I talked. If you understand those, you will see why I translated as "and perfected the Nirvana," though some scholars say it should be "reached final Nirvana" from the original Sanskrit text. The latter translation has no sense of "to live among the people for saving them." Perfect wisdom means perfect love, and Nirvana will be perfected by both. There is no place to reach; from the beginning we are here, here only we will or will not perfect Nirvana. Entering into Nirvana means to work sincerely without expecting any result. If you are a soldier, drill from morning until night; if you are a farmer, clean your plow all the time for cultivating; if you are a carpenter, plane the board very well; if you are a merchant, count the money correctly. Even animals are doing so every day.

Here there is a koan from *Katto-shu*:

In the preaching on Maka-hannya, Bodhisattva Monju said, "A

Freedom, The Life of No Attainment

pure trainer does not enter into Nirvana, but a priest who violates the commandments does not fall into Hell."

What is the meaning of "A pure trainer does not enter into Nirvana" and "a priest who violates the commandments does not fall into Hell"?

> Each raindrop makes its wave in the pond.
> Dragonflies are egg laying on the root of lotus,
> Jet airplane makes a white line after rain,
> And young man runs away by motorcycle
> Like a thread on the pondside.

Well, Bodhisattva Avalokitesvara perfected Nirvana, without getting anything but by only awakening the mind of "no attainment." This means we have already Nirvana in ourselves. If we practice the paramitas, we can awaken to this fact. Don't misunderstand that you can get something by training. You cannot get anything. If you train very well, you can prove there is Nirvana but you cannot make it. You can use it but you cannot create it.

> A monk asked Priest Seijo, "Why could not Mahābhijñājñānā-bhibu-Buddha (The Full-Free-Wise-Excellent Buddha) become the Buddha even though he had meditation on the seat of the Dharma while ten kalpas passed?, and why was the Dharma not presented in front of him?"

If I say simply the same thing, "Why can't I, being the universe itself and being in the freedom and being the incomparably wise one, become God even though I have been having meditation as Buddha since the beginning of the universe? and why was the Dharma not presented in front of me?"

Priest Seijo answered, "Your question itself is the great answer."

Unfortunately this monk could not understand the kindly answer and asked further,

> "Already he was sitting on the seat of Buddha. Why could he not become Buddha?"

Priest Seijo will not explain any more, it will only make worse confusion for the monk. And he says,

> "Yes, he will not become Buddha eternally."

Is this saying kindly or cruel for you? I also will not explain any more. While you don't understand this, you are Buddha. If you understand this, you are an ignorant man. Don't try to pick a flower up with your hand and so doing, kill it. After you kill the flower, even though you try to make beautiful art such as Zen flower arrangement, it makes only the cause to enter into the hell. Indeed I don't agree that flower arrangement is good Japanese Zen culture. It is not Zennist's work at all. Tea ceremony has also very dangerous weak points. Swordsmanship also. For me the sorrowful thing is that many people think those are Zen culture and done by Zen lives. I don't think so. They are playing in the ideal without knowing they are playing on the dangerous cliff. In Japanese Zen culture there is no Zen. Zen culture was one past step of the process of Zen, died already. About these maybe I should talk on another occasion. Anyway, when a Zennist begins to have so much interest in such Zen culture, already he is stopping his life as a Zennist. Culture itself is the dust which was not the purpose of Zen, or Religion. Who is admiring sincerely the pyramids? It was one of the most foolish things in the history of human beings. If I have such authority, power, time and laborers, will I build such strange useless forms? Building a school is much more worthwhile. Zen culture also is like a pyramid. Don't try to enter into such a tomb.

XI Anuttara-samyak-sambodhi

All Buddhas of the three worlds live in Prajna-paramita; therefore they get Anuttara-samyak sambodhi. Therefore we should know the Prajna-paramita is the great mysterious Mantram, the great wisdom Mantram, the great supreme Mantram, the great peerless Mantram which can remove all sufferings very well; it is truth but not falsehood. Then there is the Mantram of Prajna-paramita. It said, "Gate, gate, paragate, parasamgate, bodhi, svaha!"

San ze sho butsu, e han nya ha ra mi ta ko, toku a noku ta ra sam myaku sam bo dai, ko chi han nya ha ra mi ta, ze dai jin shu, ze dai myo shu, ze mujo shu, ze mu to do shu, no jo its sai ku, shin jitsu fu ko, ko setsu han nya ha ra mi ta shu, soku setsu shu watsu, gya tei, gya tei, ha ra gya tei, ha ra so gya tei bo dhi so wa ka.

Han nya shin gyo[1]

Buddha means one who enlightened for the phenomenal world and the substance of phenomena, and perfected his humanity. This means he has awakened to our original nature which is eternity, not-be-born and not-be-ruined, and not able to be divided to two, but only one. In short, as in this Sutra, Buddha means one who lives in Prajna-paramita. Therefore there are uncountable Buddhas in this world. This world was divided into three in time, called the world of past, the world of present, and the world of future. These classifications of three worlds were made only as a kindness to blind persons who cannot see that the world is one. Always people will see the world as three in time and as thousands in space; at least they divide the world into two in space, East and West. But in fact there is only one whole world. People will see each physical phenomenon as substance. But there is not any substance. Then we should see each physical phenomenon as a momentary harmony which was observed by our imperfect organs. We cannot pick up only one phenomenon from thousands of phenomena. If we pick up even a sesame seed, already all other phenomena are moving. Because there is not a thing which has independent substance; all are depending on Cause and Effect and mutual relations.

Naturally we cannot divide the world to any number in time and in space. Then we will know this Sutra talked with the blind man's words by saying "three worlds." In fact, just as there is one world, there is one Buddha who is living in Prajna-paramita, which is our original nature. Unfortunately you cannot understand correctly these matters by only brain study without a correct teacher. While you are so, we will go on with the Sutra.

In Buddhism, the various sects are insisting on their own understanding of Buddha, Dharma, and Sangha, and abusing each other. And the same thing on a little larger scale is happening among the various faiths. For example, between Buddhism and Christism[2] there are many such fightings of parasitic worms. Though they will fight with all their sincerity, indeed they are not fighting for their own Masters but only for themselves. Let me say that if Christ fails by the Buddha it makes shame for religion, and if Buddha fails by the Christ it makes humiliation for religion. Because both are saviors of human beings. In Eastern words if I dare say, both are Buddha. In Western words it will be said that both are God. Still further you may think, why are parasitic worms of each side fighting? Because really they don't know themselves and their Masters. They don't know that wisdom is love and love is wisdom. And they don't know that the precepts are natural acts of love and wisdom.

"Therefore they get Anuttara-samyak-sambodhi" was also spoken to the blind person; in Saint Paul's expression: "I will speak after the manner of men" (Romans 3:5). They will not get anything, but they will be as Anuttara-samyak-sambodhi, which means they live in the highest perfect enlightenment, literally. In a practical sense, how are

佛

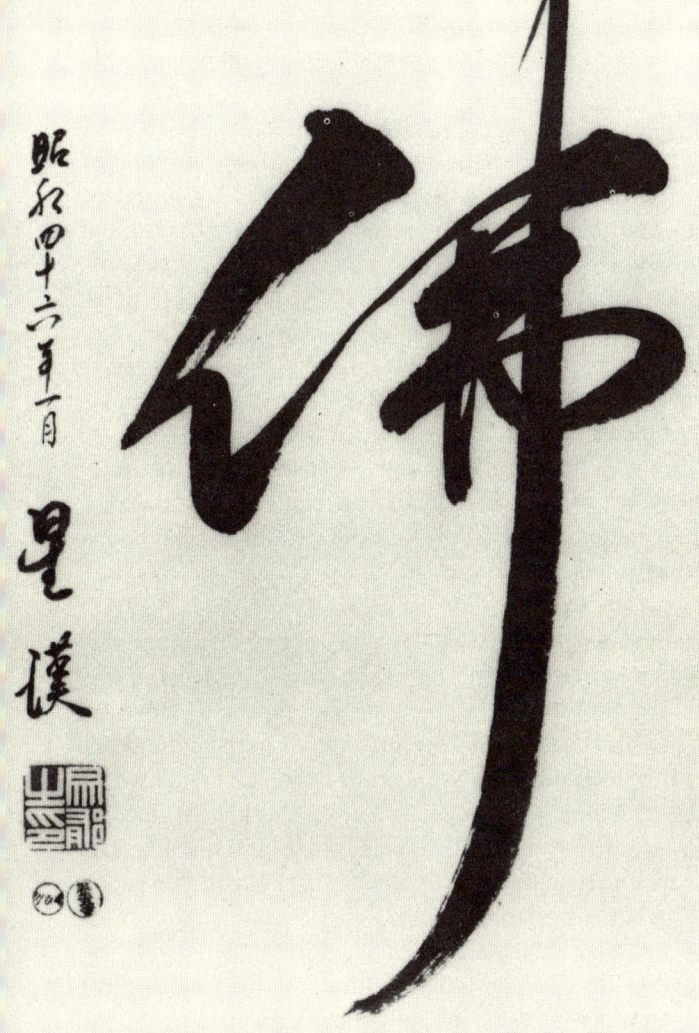

昭和四十六年一月
星漢

they living? Let me explain by introducing two stories from the *Jataka*[3] in which the humanity of Sakyamuni Buddha is made concrete. His acts of wisdom and love (which are only mysterious courage for the blind people) were described poetically.

Once upon a time when Sakyamuni Buddha was born as a king, Sivi, and was training in the Bodhisattva Way, a wounded dove flew trembling into his bosom. While the king protected and comforted the dove kindly, a hawk came to chase it and asked, looking all around,
"Just now did not a dove fly here?"
"It came here and is in my bosom," replied the king.
Hearing this reply, the dove increased its fear and began to tremble even more. The king, who was Sakyamuni Buddha, pitied and determined to help it, and comforted it, saying, "Helping all sentient beings is my vow. Then I will certainly help you also."
But the hawk, who heard these sayings, angered and appealed, crying, "No matter what, give me the dove. I am hungry. If I don't eat the dove I must starve to death."

Indeed Sakyamuni Buddha had religious fervor of mercy with sorrow, but he was faced with a complete impasse. If he gave the dove to the hawk, the dove would die, and if he tried to help the dove, the hawk would be starved to death. How did Sakyamuni Buddha decide in this case? If he had been only a teacher he might have taught to the hawk to have the mind of mercy, and said not to kill the dove, to forgive it. But he knew both of their standpoints and loved both of them. He had not time even to think such a thought. All people should study from Sakyamuni Buddha.

He asked to the hawk, "My hawk, must you eat the dove? If I can give you other meat can I help the dove and you too?"
The hawk said without any respect, "I don't eat dead meat. If you can give me the same amount of fresh meat as the dove I will be saved from starving."

The king who was Sakyamuni Buddha sliced off his thigh and compared it with the weight of the dove. It was lighter. Then he sliced off the flesh from the left side of his thigh. Still it was too light. Then he sliced off the flesh from all over his body and gave it to the hawk. The hawk could eat the fresh meat and enjoyed, and the dove could get rid of its danger and enjoyed, but from all places of Sakyamuni Buddha red fresh blood was running out. He did not care even to wipe the blood but smiled like an infant baby by seeing both lives were helped.

There is another story:

Once upon a time Sakyamuni Buddha was born as a prince, Vessantara, and was training in the Bodhisattva Way. As he grew up he was endowed with both wisdom and virtue and was filled with the mind of mercy with sorrow. He was always donating to the people who were suffering by their illness, starvation, poorness, and so on. Whenever he had time, he visited charity hospitals to comfort the pitiful people. Accordingly his merciful practice became famous in the neighboring countries. A king of a neighboring country had envy and made his servant disguise himself as a training monk and try to snatch a white elephant owned by the prince.

Prince Vessantara, seeing through the trick of the furiously desiring king, gave his white elephant without any hesitation. However, as soon as the servants of the prince heard of this happening they indignantly told the king, father of the prince. The king judged the charity of the prince as absurd conduct and blamed him and chased him out of the country, though it was not this father's wish. News of the exile was spread through all the country, and officers of the palace and public people were full of sorrow. Especially the poor people, who could live thanks to the mercy of the prince, cried with unspeakable grief. They were grieved as if they had become crazy with sorrow for the prince. The prince had a farewell ceremony for separation from his parents and rode away in a coach with his wife and two children. He left his beloved capitol, seen off by the poor people.

With his wife and children, he entered into a forest far from human habitation and became a stoical trainer. Then he walked in the forest, holding a lovely boy in his arms while the princess walked beside him pulling a pretty a girl by her hand. Fruit trees hung down their branches as if they welcomed the good guests and provided food for the princely family. A cheerful stream gave them enough water and freshness, and a richly fragrant wind was softly breezing. The path was like flower beds. Finally they reached a cottage upon a hill and it welcomed them though it was standing lonesomely far from the social world. The cottage was made with grasses and leaves just as if built by the hands of God. And this prince with his princess and two children could enjoy the happy life as host of this cottage, being free from all restraints of status and richness.

But one day a shabby looking beggar visited this cottage and said, "O prince! Your deep mercy with sorrow is so famous, echoing through all worlds, that I have heard you donated all your possessions except your wife and children to the people. But now my wife has gotten old age and is hoping to get some helpers. She would like to get your two children as her servants."

It was a very unexpected begging for the prince. But he had vowed hard to give anything to the poor people, and said calmly, "I will give my two children to you as servants to comply with your hope."

Then sitting quietly, the prince and his wife could only have worship for the safety of their lovely children. Their worship did not stop until it reached the holy seat of a goddess in heaven. The goddess was looking down upon the two human beings, a man and a woman who were the prince and princess sitting quietly at the cottage in the trainers' forest. The goddess was strongly impressed, and respected and admired them. She thought this prince sacrificed even his lovely children to others and would certainly become the highest Buddha, the Master of teaching, in the next life's world.

But had he determination to give even his beloved wife to others?

Then she tried to test the bottom of his mind about it, and the next morning she disguised herself and appeared in front of the eyes of the two persons. Without any politeness she said to them, "I have heard you gave your two children to others yesterday. Today I would like to get your beautiful princess. Can you give to me?"

The prince looked toward his wife and asked to her mind. She was understanding the vow and the real mind of the prince, so she was not surprised at all. She was not blaming or angering or thinking such matters as people do who see human beings only as material, and she sat quietly like an image.

The goddess could not stop expressing her admiration and said, "If you are not really the pure-minded person, you cannot understand and also cannot believe such mysterious conducts. But you have the vow to get no attainment and have thrown your lovely children and lovely wife away. What a great prince you are! All gods and people will respect and admire you. Anyway, the light of the moon should stay with the moon. Therefore I will give back to you your loyal wife and I will get back your children also. And you can go to the palace as a prince again."

After her prophecy she disappeared suddenly. And just such a mysterious matter happened. They were welcomed to the palace exactly as the goddess prophesied.

Both of the above stories are showing Anuttara-samyak-sambodhi or Avalokitesvara or Buddha, who are living in Prajna-paramita. Without the Prajna-paramita even if you imitate such conduct you will become only a stoic or masochist. And you will misunderstand the next sayings of the Sutra, "mysterious" and "Mantram." If you don't see your original nature, "mysterious" means simply "unscientific matter," and "Mantram" is a word of shamanism which is a product of the fear of primitive human beings. Even now many people are using these words in that sense. "Mysterious" means the absolute free world which can be testified by the practice of the Bodhisattva Way though it cannot be understood by our dualistic thinking because it is beyond any analysis and guessing. For the Bodhisattva it is common sense, as are "miracles" for him; but for the blind persons it is an unthinkable matter, as a "miracle" is for them. Our world is a mysterious thing, our mind is a mysterious thing. Try to see your own mind, you will see this mysterious thing.

"Mantram" means true word which is true practice of the Bodhisattva Way. All other things are not true words, not true Mantram. In this world there are many people who think they know the meaning of Mantram without practicing the Bodhisattva Way. If they don't practice it, their undersatnding of Mantram is not more than toxin to destroy their healthy brains. And for destroying the brain there are some people who use this word "Mantram." Of course they can get the dead quietness if they destroy their brains, just as well as those who take L.S.D. But we should be awake all the time. Real quietness will be seen in the turning top, speedily, or in the sincere worker. Therefore we can say by seeing such a great worker that he had Mantram, true word, real practice, not falsehood. Remember, please, Sakyamuni Buddha denied shamanism strongly, and denied getting the dead quietness. Without Prajna-paramita even if you get quietness you are little better than a furious beast or a crazy person in the hospital, but not better than a crow who at least works in the field. Mantram is in our mind, not outside our mind; don't be silly trying to get it from outside. If you practice the paramitas of precepts, Dhyana, and wisdom you can see the Mantram in yourself. But I will say that without these basic three practices you cannot see Mantram eternally, only you will hear from outside like the breeze of wind through pine trees.

Then you can understand the four admirations for the Mantram in this Sutra: the great mysterious, the great wisdom, the great supreme, and the great peerless Mantram. All these are admiring our original nature, our own mind which is the universe. I hope you will train in the Bodhisattva Way and live as your nature. Please know yourself about your mind. That is the only way to live as a Bodhisattva, which makes you and others really happy. All other ways are only finally making the cause to create hell on this earth.

Coming to this point, Sakyamuni Buddha could not preach any more except, "it is truth but not falsehood." But I will ask to you, what means "it is truth but not falsehood"? . . . In my own answer, "0, 1, 2," that is, "Gate, gate, paragate, parasamgate, bodhi, svaha!" Many people try to explain or translate this part while saying it should not be done, or it could not be done. Why should I show to you your eyes by gouging out your eyes? If you like to know those literal meanings, go to another book, but don't become a summer moth which goes close to the fire and is burned by himself.

The Four Vows of Zen Buddhism

Shigu-seigan-mon[4]

Ah, indeed there are innumerable sentient beings
    inside and outside of me.
But I vow to save them.
This is my energy, and why I am living.

However, when I see the passions,
    how inexhaustible they are!
Still I vow to cut them off.
How?
KA!

It is very fortunate that the Dharmas
    are immeasurable.
Of course I vow to enjoy all of them.

The Buddha Way is the highest,
I vow to attain it.

Notes

A Note on Spelling: Sanskrit, Chinese, and Japanese words are printed with their appropriate diacritical marks and in italics *(persons' names in roman) when they are first introduced in the text, and in the index. Elsewhere they are treated as English.*

Notes to the Preface

p. 1   1. A Zen phrase. Zen phrases are collected from many records of Zennists' sayings or writings. "There are many people who preach the truth, but there are few who live it," is the companion of this phrase.

p. 1   2. Or "thusness." These are translations of the Japanese word *nyo,* or *tathatā* in Sanskrit. I hope you will understand what is meant by this word suchness as you read this book. Meanwhile you can think of suchness as "itself" or "truth before we think of it."

p. 1   3. William Smith Clark (1826–1886) said, "Boys be ambitious!" to his students when he went to Japan in 1876 to establish the Imperial College of Agriculture at Sapporo. This American's words continued to stir Japanese youth until quite recently. Modern Japanese civilization is not a little the result of his words of spiritual encouragement.

p. 1   4. Until the Meiji Restoration (1868) there were four different ranks of people. Samurai is a general word for the privileged classes, warriors, governors, and scholars. Literally, samurai describes "those who live only for others' happiness without ego, but with wisdom and morality."

Notes to the two stanzas

p. 3　　1. Before we open and chant any sutra, we chant this short Chinese quatrain. If we study a sutra with the mind of this stanza, it is certain we will get real rewards. Even if you stand in front of a beautiful meadow and forest, if your attitude is an evil one you will change them into a burned battlefield.

The first phrase expresses devout respect, love and trust for the Law. This is the mind of the person who seeks the truth.

The second phrase expresses profound thanks to Cause and Effect. Numerous people and things throughout ages (kalpas) past have made it possible to open the sutra now. This phrase expresses gratitude to the being of beings.

Just like the pure enjoyment of a baby when he gets milk, we simply enjoy the fact of the third phrase.

Indeed, what can we say except to vow, in this moment, to study harder and further. This mind itself is the Tathagatha, or Buddha or God. But if we stop at this step, the Tathagatha will die. We will seek the Tathagatha more and more. Then the Tathagatha will live more and more.

p. 3　　2. This poem I made in accordance with the custom by which lecturers of the priesthood will make their own stanza when they begin to preach. By the way, from now on when poems and translations occur without mention of the author's name, they were made by me.

Notes to Chapter I

p. 4　　1. A part of the enormous Buddhist canon. This part

168 THE CAVE OF POISON GRASS

p. 4   devoted to wisdom is called in English *The Great Wisdom Sutra.* It consists of six hundred volumes.

p. 4   2. Such as funerals, memorial services, weddings, completion ceremonies, etc.

p. 4   3. There are hundreds of lectures or commentaries on the Hannya-shin-gyo. The following are classically important lecturers in Japan: Chiko, Saicho, Shinko, Genshin, Ikkyu, Enni, Shosen, Denson, Hakuin, Enji, Kukai, Kakuban, Dohan, Raiyu, Koho, etc. Among the authors of recent publications, Zenji Kosen Imakita, Rev. Kakusho Takagami, and Rev. Kyojun Shimizudani are great helpers for making this sutra understandable. On this occasion I will have pure thanks to all of these persons.

p. 4   4. Avalokitesvara is referred to in Japanese as Kannon (Kwannon). For Buddhists Avalokitesvara is as Mary, the Virgin Mother is for Catholics. For a more detailed understanding, see Chapter III.

p. 4   5. *Manual of Zen Buddhism* (New York, Grove Press. 1960). I have been able to study from this book for my English translations.

p. 5   6. Hsuan-chuang's description of his travels has given me great encouragement. It exists in English translation: *Ta-t'ang-hsi-yü-chi, Buddhist Records of the Western World,* translated by Samuel Beal (London, 1884; Boston, 1885).

p. 6   7. The oldest existing Sanskrit text in the world is kept in Shoso-in at Nara, Japan.

Notes to Chapter II

p. 8   1. The period when Nara, south of Kyoto, was the Japanese capitol, 710–794.

p. 8   2. When the center of political power was in Kyoto, 794–1192.

p. 10   3. A great person tends to be deified by his worshipers.

To know the original person, we should study his biography. The personality attributed to him by tradition tells us about his worshipers. Both history and tradition have meaning, but should not be mixed. In this context, Bodhidharma will be described as he was traditionally represented.

p. 10　　4. A kind of Inka-shomei.

p. 11　　5. In Chinese, Hui-k'o.

p. 12　　6. Points we should make clear, usually made from the dialogue between Zen Teachers and disciples.

p. 12　　7. In Chinese, Nan-ch'üan P'u-yüan (748–834). This koan is in the collection entitled *Mumon-kan (Gateless Gate)*. This collection is one of the most important Zen text books, edited by Mumon Ekai (Wumên Hui-k'ai, 1183–1260, Southern Sung Dynasty) who collected for this work forty-eight koans and composed a commentary and stanza for each one.

p. 16　　8. Lecture is the interpretation of what is written in the text; teisho is showing the mind of the text, or pointing higher than the text. Dialogue is to make us understand the truth by the discriminating intelligence. Sanzen is without the interference of any discrimination, but only the reflecting of truth, like two mirrors facing each other. Dialogue depends on words, but for sanzen words are not essential.

p. 17　　9. Spoken English is much better than Japanese about expressing respect, modesty and politeness because while Japanese has many words to express these things, English has very few. That means English speaking people must resort to expressing these by the sound and by the real mind rather than by the play of words.

p. 19　　10. Hakuin Ekaku (1685–1768). He could say these words, which are also the declaration of perfect democracy, at a time of severe feudalism in Japan.

Sakyamuni Buddha said similar words in about 400 B.C. in India.

p. 20   11. In Chinese, Lin-chi I-hsuan (d. 867).

p. 21   12. An imaginary person who is the most important figure in the *Vimalakīrti Nirdeśa Sutra*. Now there is an English translation by Charles Luk, published by Shambala Press, Berkeley, 1972.

p. 22   13. See note 7.

p. 22   14. In Chinese, Hui-nêng (638–713).

p. 22   15. In fact, we cannot divide life and death. So to express this fact I write "life-and-death." For Buddhists life and death are two aspects of one thing.

p. 24   16. From *Byosho-rokushaku* (*The Sickbed Six Feet Long*) by Shiki Masaoka (no English translation). In the late nineteenth century he revived Haiku literature, which had been on the decline since the Basho epoch two hundred years before.

Notes to Chapter III

p. 31   1. A translation from the Japanese noun *semui*. It has two meanings. One is "to donate fearlessness," the other "to donate fearlessly."

p. 39   2. Translation by Dr. Daisetsu T. Suzuki.

p. 39   3. Take note of the teaching of Sakyamuni Buddha: "Let people confess but make sure people do not have regret or guilt for their sin."

p. 48   4. Kamikaze literally means "the wind given by God." Though almost every year the Japanese suffer from typhoons, their winds occasionally protected them from attack by foreign navies in the past.

p. 54   5. When I translated these from Chinese, the translation to modern Japanese made by Dr. Jikai Fujiyoshi was very helpful to me. He deserves full respect and thanks.

Notes   171

p. 61   6. *Hekigan-roku* (in Chinese *Pi-yen-lu*), *The Records of Blue Rock Temple,* consists of one hundred koans collected by the Zen priest Setcho (Hsüeh-tou, 980–1052) in the Sung Dynasty, and commented on by Engo (Yüan-wu, 1063–1175) in the Ming Dynasty. It is one of seven important collections for the Zen sect. Parts of it have been translated into English by various writers.

p. 61   7. Sanzen literally means "to study Zen." Here it is used to mean "to study under a Zen teacher in a private room." See also Chapter II, note 8.

p. 67   8. See Chapter IX, note 1.

p. 68   9. Dr. Suzuki's book *Zen and Japanese Culture.* By the way, it is very interesting to think of the saying of Kaishu Katsu who studied Zen and was also a great teacher of swordsmanship in the nineteenth century. He said, "Without depending on Zen, swordsmanship can be done very well." Certainly, I would like to say, if swordsmanship means "the art to kill life," then Zen has nothing to do with it.

p. 73   10. See Chapter IX note 1.

p. 75   11. Frankly I don't know about the Sanskrit more than this. If you are interested in this subject, please see other books, especially *Kan-ze-on-bosatsu no ken-kyu* (*The Study of Avalokitesvara*) written by Dr. Daiyu Goto (Tokyo, 1958), not translated into English.

p. 76   12. In my belief the Resurrection of Christ occurred when he died on the Cross, not later. When I think that both happened at once, the meaning of the Cross becomes really important and relevant to our daily life, instead of mysterious and symbolic.

Notes to Chapter IV

p. 86   1. Kṣitigarbha in Sanskrit. Between the death of Sakyamuni Buddha and the appearance of Maitreya

172   THE CAVE OF POISON GRASS

(5,670,000,000 years after Buddha's death), this Jizo Bodhisattva will help sentient beings, according to traditional Buddhist theory. Here he is considered as a god for children.

p. 90   2. When the great Japanese Haiku poet Basho (1644–1694) was on his deathbed his disciples asked him to leave some last word. replied, "Don't be silly, my every day poems are my last words."

Notes to Chapter V

p. 94   1. I am sorry that English does not allow me to write "All beings will be born and *will be died.*" Because this form of the verb is more accurate according to Buddhist philosophy of life.

p. 100   2. This collection, also, has been only partly translated into English. Joshu Jushin (Chao-chou Ts'ung-shên, 778–897) was a Zen priest of the T'ang Dynasty, the Tenth Chinese Patriarch in Zen transmission.

Notes to Chapter VI

p. 108   1. I think understanding that there were chiefly ten groups under these ten unsurpassed disciples is more historically accurate than simply thinking that there were ten disciples.

p. 108   2. Maha-kasyapa is the one who inherited the seat of Sakyamuni Buddha after his death.

One day Buddha took his lecture seat in front of thousands of disciples and laymen. Unlike the usual lecture, he kept silent and just held up a flower. No one could be sure what Buddha meant by his quiet act except Maha-kasyapa, who smiled like a baby in its mother's arms. Buddha declared, "I have the teaching of the mysterious and miraculous Law of form and formless form; it is the essence of perfect freedom, it is the eye to see all truth and falsehood. Now I have passed this on to Maha-kasyapa without relying upon limited words but by direct communication."

This story is the fiction of a later age, not historical fact. But Zen Buddhists believe the essence of Buddhism is declared in this story. So the Zen Sect will often be called the "Buddha-mind Sect."

p. 108   3. Rahula was the physical child of Siddhārtha Gautama. The latter came to be called Sakyamuni Buddha, meaning the sage who came from the Sakya Clan. As was usual for the child of a distinguished father, Rahula was treated as a special person. Nevertheless, he did not use his special position to live an easy life. On the contrary, he became a very moral person and even his father could admire him truly. By the way, the name Rahula means "obstacle." We can understand how Buddha thought, before he began to train, about marriage and having children.

p. 109   4. *Yacho-ki* (*The Record of Wild Birds*), untranslated.

p. 111   5. In Sanskrit, *Vajracchedikā-prajñā-pāramitā-sūtra*. This sutra shows the basic logic of Buddhism: 'A is not A, therefore A is A'. If I explain enlightenment logically, this "not" and "therefore" are the subjects to be enlightened to.

p. 111   6. Gyoki (d. 749) travelled through all of Japan and contributed to society by digging ponds, building levees and bridges, opening roads, etc.

p. 111   7. *Bumo-onju-kyō,* a sutra about the love of parents, describes these with illustrations quite fully.

p. 114   8. This sutra was written by the followers of the Sixth Patriarch Eno to prove their school of Zen was better or more authorized than the contemporary Jinshu school. So we should read it with fairness for both sides.

Notes to Chapter VII

p. 121   1. Musashi was a thick, wild forest and field about one hundred years ago. Now it is a thick and tall forest of buildings as a part of Tokyo.

p. 121   2. Yamato is an old name for Japan. So "spirit of Yamato" means literally "Japanese spirit." But when we understand Yamato in more detail it really means "the Great Friendship," which was one name of Japan. In the Second World War, a huge battleship was built and named "Yamato." This shows how crazily stupid the Japanese military was. This battleship was sent to the bottom quickly by the American navy. It was very well done. But people shouldn't sink the real Yamato.

p. 122   3. This "each moment" is not the present separated from the past and future as some pleasure-seekers think. It is the top of times, giving life to the past and future by denying the present, by the act of doing one's best.

Notes to Chapter VIII

p. 130   1. The most important record of the sayings of the partriarchs for the Rinzai school of Zen Buddhism.

p. 131   2. Klesa is a word for the opposite of satori or enlightenment. So it is a general name for those mental acts which cause suffering, worry, delusion, illusion, disturbance, confusion, degradation, etc. of our mind and body.

Notes to Chapter IX

p. 134   1. In Chinese Zen transmission, Zenji Hyakujo is traditionally considered the Ninth Patriarch of the Rinzai line, as you can see by the following diagram:

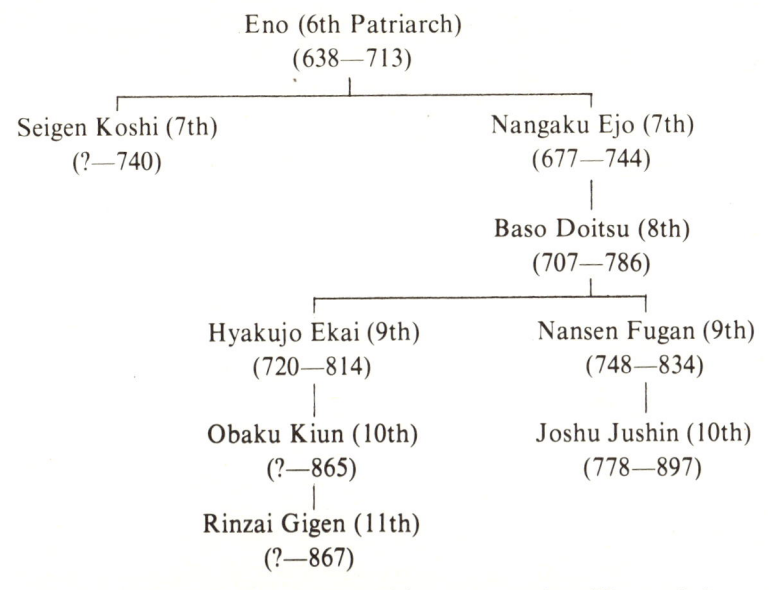

```
                    Eno (6th Patriarch)
                        (638—713)
         ┌──────────────────┴──────────────────┐
Seigen Koshi (7th)                    Nangaku Ejo (7th)
    (?—740)                               (677—744)
                                              │
                                      Baso Doitsu (8th)
                                         (707—786)
                              ┌──────────────┴──────────────┐
                      Hyakujo Ekai (9th)             Nansen Fugan (9th)
                         (720—814)                     (748—834)
                              │                             │
                      Obaku Kiun (10th)             Joshu Jushin (10th)
                          (?—865)                      (778—897)
                              │
                      Rinzai Gigen (11th)
                          (?—867)
```

p. 135   2. An officer in Buddhist monasteries. His work is to maintain the traditional schedule of monastery life.

p. 135   3. In the Zen monastery if a monk becomes sick he enters into this hall or room where he should reflect on why he got illness and observe Cause and Effect.

p. 136   4. A collection of koans, very little of which is translated. The title can also be translated as *The Collection of the Conflict*.

p. 141   5. Untranslated. Musashi Miyamoto (1584–1645) says in this book that he fought with a real sword more than sixty times and never lost once.

Notes to Chapter X

p. 152   1. Sanskrit for "the world in which we must have patience to live." This is so because inside our bodies we have various klesas, and outside we have sufferings coming from many severe conditions. In Japan, prisoners call our social world "saha."

p. 154   2. *Mushu-no-Hoetsu* (Tokyo, 1971), untranslated.

Notes to Chapter XI

p. 157   1. When we chant this sutra, we finish by chanting the title, "Han nya shin gyo," because it makes the sound of the ending more rhythmically satisfying.

p. 158   2. I don't like the word "Buddhism" in English. It is not an "-ism" at all. The same thing can be said for Christianity when we use the word "Christism." "-ism" has a narrow sort of sectarian and egotistical feeling. It greatly limits religion. "-ism" expresses only one aspect of the philosophical or moral discipline of a religion. I suggest we use the word "Buddha-life" instead of "Buddhism."

p. 160   3. The collection of stories about the former lives of Sakyamuni Buddha as various Bodhisattvas who helped many sentient beings. Folk tradition and Buddhism joined in about the third century B.C. and made these Jataka. They had a great influence on fables around the world, such as those of Aesop, and the Tales of 1001 Nights.

p. 165   4. Whereas Kai-kyo-ge is traditionally used for opening the chanting of sutras, Shigu-seigan-mon is traditionally used to close the chanting. Both are Chinese quatrains.

    The translation which follows is more loyal to the original in its literal sense. However at the close of Chapter XI, I have given my active understanding.

> Though there are innumerable sentient beings
>   I vow to help them.
> Though there are inexhaustible klesas
>   I vow to cut them,
> Though there are immeasurable Dharmas
>   I vow to master them,
> The Buddha Way is unsurpassed
>   I vow to attain it.

Indexes

Subject Index

absoluteness 113
Analytical Way 94, 96, 98
Anuttara-samyak-saṃbodhi 15, 168, 169
Atman 65–66
Bodhi 29, 98, 114–117
Bodhisattva 8, 9, 21, Ch. III, 29–30, 82, 103, 118, 137, 163, 176n
Brahman 65–66
Buddha 19–20, 23, 24, 28, 30, 39–40, 56, 62, 67, 73, 97, 100–101, 127, 144, 149, 155–159, 163, 167n
Buddha-mind seal 10, 169n
Cause and Effect 11, 39, 63, 67, 83, 92–94, 96–97, 124, 128, 134–136, 158, 167n, 175n
Cave of Poison Grass 89, 145
Ch'in 67–68
Christianity 22, 76, 88, 144, 154, 158, 168, 171n, 176n
Confucianism 10, 25, 43–44
Cross 3, 76, 98, 123, 136, 171n
Dāna-pāramitā 3n34, 41, 170n
Dan-ken 11, 24
dhāraṇī 14–15
Dharma 16, 40, 62, 65, 81–83, 94, 96–98, 118, 152, 165
Dhyāna-pāramitā 14, 31, 65–74, 150
discrimination 16, 18, 22, 82, 98–99, 101, 102, 169n
dualism 12, 16, 53, 66, 67, 69, 98, 148, 163
ego 30, 33, 35, 38, 40, 69, 117, 129, 132, 137, 152, 167n

Eight Correct Ways 140–142
emptiness 81, 83–84, 89, Ch. V, 110, 113, Ch. VII, 124, 130, 133, 136–137, 142
enlightenment 9, 15, 17, 19–20, 23–24, 25–27, 29, 42, 48, 53, 54–65, 89, 95, 97–98, 101, 131–132, 135, 145, 157
Fifteen Kinds of Good Death 78
Fifteen Kinds of Evil Death 77–78
Five Kinds of untranslatable words 12–16
Five Skandhas 81–83, 96
formless form 12, 81, 98, 134, 173n
Four Delusions 151
Four Sufferings 44–45, 94, 138
Four Truths 138–143
God 11, 17, 38, 75, 76, 82, 139, 147–148, 152, 155, 168n
Hannya (Prajñā-pāramitā) 12–14, 17–20, 39, 75, 110
Haramita (Pāramitā) 20–22
Hineyana Buddhism 21, 94–98
Inka-shomei 9, 48, 169n
Jisso-hannya 20
Jo-ken 11, 24
kaihan 60–61
kalpa 3, 155, 168n
Kansho-hannya 20
karma 39, 94, 96–97, 100, 111, 130
kleśa 20, 96–97, 131, 139, 142, 174n, 175n
koan 12, 103, 169n, 171n
Ksanti-pāramitā 31, 44–57
ku-yaku 5

Law 3, 8–9, 17, 23, 25, 31, 34, 35, 38, 43, 57, 65–66, 83–84, 114, 120, 125, 168n
Mahayana Buddhism 20–21, 92, 94–98
Maka 10–14
māna 41
Mantram 163–164
Mercy 30, 43, 50, 75, 77, 79, 160–161
Middle Way 11, 113
mind 10–12, 24, 38, 62, 67, 76, 81, 82, 100, 119, 149–150, 164, 173n
Moji-hannya 20
Mu 11, 57, Ch. V, 99–107
mutual relation 38, 67, 72, 96, 124, 126, 128, 158
nihilism 11, 24, 42, 139
Nirvāṇa 21, 22–23, 29, 30, 51–52, 69, 154–155
Pāramitā 21, 22, 31, 68, 75, 150, 164
pilgrimage 18, 46, 104, 108, 126 (illustration 47)
Prajñā-pāramitā 12, 14, 17, 20, 31, 67, 68, 75–79, 134, 150, 157–158, 163–164
relativity 16, 113
religion 15, 16–18, 32, 34, 50, 52, 97, 113, 118, 128, 133, 141, 154, 156, 158, 176n
Roshi 9, 16–17, 48
Sahā 152, 175n
samadhi 14, 28, 64, 67, 71, 74
samurai 1, 11, 166n
Sangha 39, 158
sanzen 16, 61, 169n, 171n

science 15, 31, 50, 83, 118
shin 24
shin-yaku 5
Śilā-pāramitā 31, 35–45, 67, 89, 99
stoicism 70, 144, 163
suchness 1, 16, 18, 20, 75, 117, 134, 166n
Śūnyatā 89, Ch. V, 110, 113–117, Ch. VII
sutra 8, 24–25, 28, 29, 77, 168
Synthetic Way 94, 97–98
Taoism 10, 25, 102
Tathāgatha 3, 166n, 168n
Ten Disciples 108–109, 172n, 173n
Ten Precepts 40–43
teisho 16, 169n
Therevada Buddhism 21
Three Poisons 19, 39
Three Purities for Donation 31
Three Treasures 39–40, 43
Three Worlds 93, 138–139, 157–158
training 5, 9, 15, 17, 18, 30, 33–34, 36, 40, 46–48, 54–66, 70–72, 97, 99, 101–103, 118, 122, 128, 144–145, 150, 153–156
Twelve Steps of Cause and Effect 93–94, 134
U 11, 12, 90, 100–101, 102, 105
Virya-pāramitā 31, 51-65
zazen 10, 66–74
Zen 12, 16, 20, 23–24, 46, 52–53, 65–68, 71, 99–100, 103, 156, 166, 171n, 173n, 174n
Zenji 16–17

Index of Names

Aristotle 94
Avalokiteśvara (Kannon) 4, 8, 29, 50, 75–79, 80, 152–154, 163, 168n, 171n
Basho 170, 172n
Baso Doitsu 61, 73, 175n
Berkeley 94
Bodhidharma 10–11, 57, 142–144, (illustrations 58, 143)
Descartes 94
Diogenes 153
Eka 10–11, 169n
Eno 22, 67, 114–117, 170n, 173n (illustration 115)
Hakuin Ekaku 19, 99, 103, 122, 168, 169 (illustration 143)
Hotei 147
Hsüan-chuang 5–6, 12, 168n
Hume 94
Hyakujo Ekai 67, 134–136, 174n
Ikkyu, 168n
Imakita, Kosen 103–107, 168n
Jinshu 114–117
Jizo Bodhisattva 86, 171n–172n
Joshu Jushin 57, 65, 100–102, 104, 144, 175n
Kajiura, Itsugai 25–28, 31, 36–37, 123
Kant 79, 94

Kumārajīva 4–5
Kyogen 25 (illustration 26)
Mahā-kāśyapa 108, 173n
Maitreya 171
Marx 139
Miyamoto Musashi 140, 175n
Monju Bodhisattva 16, 19, 21
Mujinni Bodhisattva 76, 152
Mumon Ekai 31, 101–102, 169n
Nansen Fugan 12, 62, 67, 99, 169n, 175 (illustration 13)
Rāhula 108, 173n
Rinzai Gigen 20, 55, 130–133, 170n, 174n–175n
Śākyamuni Buddha 5, 8, 10, 12, 25, 29, 42, 44–46, 66–81, 93–94, 96, 99, 100, 108–109, 124, 125, 160, 163, 170n, 173
Santa Claus 147
Śāriputra 92, 108–109
Shido Bunan 23
Shoju 137
Spinoza 94
Suzuki, Daisetz 4, 168n, 170n, 171n
Unsei Renchi 52
Vimalakīrti 21, 170n

Index of Buddhist Sutras, Zen Koans, and Related Texts

Baso Doitsu Zenji Goroku (Records of the Sayings of Zenji Baso Doitsu) 61
Bumo-onju-kyō 173n
Byosho-rokushaku (The Sickbed Six Feet Long) 24, 170n
Daihi-shu (Great Mercy With The Sorrow Dharani Sutra) 77
Daihōkō-butsu-kegon-kyō (Kegon-kyō) 8, 18
Den-to-roku (Record of the Transmission of the Lamp) 72
Go-rin-sho (The Book of Five Wheels) 140–141
Hekigan-roku (The Records of Blue Rock Temple) 61, 65, 99, 123, 170n
Jātaka 160–163, 176n
Joshu Shinzai Zenji Goroku (The Sayings of Zenji Joshu Shinzai) 65, 100, 173n
Kai-kyō-ge ("Stanza for Opening the Sutras") 3, 166n, 176n
Katto-shu (Mingling Vines of Ivy and Wisteria: Koan Collection) 136, 154–155, 175n
koans 12, 22, 24, 43–44, 57, 61, 62, 65, 99, 100–107, 112, 122, 134–138, 147–150, 154–156
Madhyamāgama Sutra 44–46
Mahāprajñāpāramitā Sutra 4–6, 24, 167n–168n
Maka-hannya-haramita-shin-gyō (Hannya-shin-gyo, Hannya Sutra) 4–8, 10, 29, 92, 108–109, 168n, 176n
Muji-no-uta ("Song of Mu") 103–107
Mumon-kan (Gateless Gate) 22, 24, 62, 101–103, 134–136, 169n
Mushu-no-hoetsu (The Enjoyment of Dharma Without Hands) 153–154
Myōhō-renge-kyō (Hokke-kyō, Lotus Flower Sutra) 8–10, 76–77, 138, 152
Nirvana Sutra 100
San-ge-mon ("Sentences of Confession") 39, 170n
San-ki-kai ("The Precepts for Believing the Three Treasures") 40
Shichi-butsu-ge ("The Teaching of the Seven Buddhas") 38
Shigu-seigan-mon ("The Four Vows") 166, 176n
Shodo-ka ("The Song of Proving the Way") 63
Sixth Patriarch's Sutra 67, 114–117, 173n
Sutra of Metaphor 139–140
Ta-k'ang-hsi-yü-chi (Buddhist records of the Western World) 4, 5, 168n
Vajracchedikā-prajñā-pāramitā Sutra (Diamond Prajna Sutra) 111, 149–150, 173n
Vimalakīrti Nirdeśa Sutra (Yuima-kyō) 9, 21
Zen-ju-i-ten-shi-sho-mon-kyō 16
Zen-kan-saku-shin (The Whips to Get Through Zen Borders) 52–65, 70

About the Author

Seikan Hasegawa was born in a Zen Buddhist temple in a suburb of Kyoto in 1945, just after the end of World War II. His grandfather was a well known Zen Buddhist priest, vice abbot of one Zen Buddhist head temple, Nanzen-ji in Kyoto. His father was also a Zen Buddhist priest, who mastered the art of calligraphy and enjoyed an artist's life.

His family's temple, Yogen-ji, had possessed a large amount of land like an old feudal estate, and until the war his family had lived a comfortable, artistic and spiritual life. However they lost their land and tenants under the decree of General MacArthur as part of the policy of occupation. Thus he grew up in a situation where from the time he was born he had to ask himself the questions, what is life? what is desire? how should we live? why can't we live without war? Fortunately he could sustain himself by getting food from the offerings made by laymen to the tombs in the graveyard, and could study many things from his father.

At age fourteen he officially entered into the priesthood and was registered as an acolyte Zen priest at Nanzen-ji. While attending public school he kept Buddhist morality and studied the basic theory, history and art of Buddhism under his father and the senior priest of Nanzen-ji. At age nineteen he was well prepared to train as a Zen monk. He chose what was known as the best Zen training monastery, Shogen-ji in Gifu Prefecture. His Zen Master was Itsugai Kajiura who is now the abbot of another head Zen temple, Myoshin-ji. The most important thing for training as a Zennist is koan study. Rev. Hasegawa completed all his koan study in the extraordinarily short time of four years and was certified as a Zen Master by his teacher.

Rather than using the social rank or title of Zen Master, he continued further study by himself, traveling all over Japan on foot. After one year he wanted to study Southern Buddhism as well as Northern Buddhism. So in 1969, at the age of twenty-four, he went to Thailand and was ordained as a Thai monk. While he was there he concluded that one of the most important ways to attain world peace is to promote understanding between East and West. Reflecting on his study and experience, he decided he should spend all his life to introduce Buddhism, the religion, philosophy, morality and art of Eastern people, to Westerners. Like his grandfather, who had wanted to come to America for the same purpose but had died before he could fulfill that dream, he believed Americans are the people most capable of understanding Buddhism, and that America can absorb Buddhism to make something more than just Buddhism or just Christianity, something which is really the useful truth for everyone on this earth.

Thus he came to America in 1969 and since then has formed the Rock Creek Buddhist Temple of America, a religious corporation, in Maryland, near Washington, D.C. One of the earliest supporters of his efforts was Rev. Joshu Sasaki, who has been in America many years as Zen Master in Los Angeles, and is now a trustee of Rock Creek Buddhist Temple. Rev. Hasegawa is currently teaching both in the U.S. and Japan, teaching Zen Buddhism and Japanese culture, especially the arts of painting and calligraphy, to Americans, and introducing American culture to Japanese. He and his wife, who is American, were married in 1970 and have one son.

The Cave of Poison Grass was written as a part of the author's life work. In it he has set out to express the essence of Buddhism, and the book serves as a foundation for other works he is now writing and planning. He welcomes correspondence, which may be addressed to him at **Rock Creek Buddhist Temple of America (738 South 22 St., Arlington, Virginia 22202) or Yogen-ji (14 Inokura, Miyazaki-cho, Kameoka-shi, Kyoto, Japan 621-02).**